OUT OF THE RUINS

Pioneer Life in Frontier Phoenix, Arizona Territory 1867–1881

Patrick Grady

Out of the Ruins

Library of Congress Control Number: 2011918806
ISBN 978-0-615-55511-9

Arizona Pioneer Press
P. O. Box 306
Cave Creek, Arizona 85327

TABLE OF CONTENTS

PREFACE

Phoenix, 2012. One hundred years after Statehood. One hundred and forty-five years from Anglo/Mexican settlement along the Salt River. A City population in the 1.5 million range. A metropolitan population exceeding 4 million, stretching in all directions in never-ceasing, tile roof subdivisions. The Salt River, once a lush, life-giving riparian corridor; now, captured in a series of dams and recreational lakes prior to its waters being carried in concrete channels for domestic distribution. The frontier past of Phoenix is all but forgotten, so distant a memory, amidst the growth of the Salt River Valley.

Yet, the early frontier history of Phoenix is an important chapter in the legendary settlement of the Southwest. This was not a Kansas cattle town. Nor was it a rough and wild mining town of western lore, as characterized by Tombstone. It did not have the historic Spanish influence of Santa Fe or Tucson.

This is a story of frontier life rooted in agriculture, sustained by the Salt River. It is a story of how Anglo and Mexican settlers prevailed to create a community out of the ruins of the earlier Hohokam civilization, in the oft-inhospitable environment of the Sonoran Desert. Frontier Phoenix embodies the western settlement patterns of competition, boosterism, land speculation and growth, and most importantly, capturing and managing the natural resource of water. Its early land use and growth set the pattern for Phoenix development for the next century. Its agricultural base would dominate the local economy well into the 20th century.

The growth of the settlement of Phoenix resulted from a number of influences, with canal development and the success of agriculture being preeminent. While life certainly revolved around the farm, the story of the establishment of the Phoenix Townsite is a classic case study of local Western politics, including a gunfight between opposing candidates for Sheriff. Sketches of town life provides a glimpse into how settlers lived and socialized within the young and growing community.

Many of these early pioneers are long forgotten. There are no monuments commemorating the pioneer spirit of those times. Even the Phoenix Museum of History recently closed. With a couple of exceptions, including Osborn Road and the Cartwright and Balsz School Districts, there are few place names memorializing early leaders. It is not likely that students of the Wilson Elementary School know that Gordon Wilson was an early canal builder and farmer. Only the founder, Jack Swilling, has received any substantive biographical treatment. Accordingly, the book profiles a number of Phoenix pioneers worthy of remembrance - William Hancock, John Alsap, Columbus Gray, Enrique Garfias, Jesus Otero, to name a few.

Homesteading had a significant, but generally poorly acknowledged, role in the development of the Arizona Territory, including Phoenix and the Salt River Valley. Generous federal land programs were a catalyst to early settlement. Another catalyst were the merchants of Washington Street, providing needed consumer goods to bring a civilizing influence to early pioneer life. One of those early merchants was George Loring; his journey is a poignant story of duty, fortune and love on the frontier. The letters of George and Aggie Loring are revealing letters, published for the first time.

And what story of life in the West would be complete without an examination of law and order in the fledgling town of Phoenix? Saloons, murder, gunfights and lynchings are a part of the frontier story. The summer of 1879 was a particularly violent year, resulting in one prisoner shot to death and two others lynched for their crimes. And crime in Phoenix was not restricted to the stereotypical outlaw.

Pioneer life in frontier Phoenix is a story worth telling. Capturing the spirit and rhythm of the community can be elusive. This collection of stories is a biography of the town, describing its contextual history, its people and their purpose, and its maturation process. The trials, tribulations and tedium are all portrayed in this small, but complex and diverse community. Even some town secrets, overlooked or simply ignored by earlier historians, are revealed. The story of early Phoenix is comprised of all these colors. In a brief fourteen years, 1867 to 1881, the frontier era was largely over. Yet, today's residents of Phoenix owe much to the legacy left by the early resilient and persevering settlers of frontier Phoenix. Their stories are worth preserving.

ACKNOWLEDGEMENTS

The historian of early Phoenix is confronted with a serious lack of traditional contemporary resources - no local newspaper until 1878, few reminiscences of quality, and no local history museum with archival resources. Many thanks, therefore, to the staff at various libraries and research repositories - Phoenix Public Library, Arizona State University, University of Arizona, Arizona State Archives and Library, the Arizona Historical Foundation, the Arizona Historical Society, and the archaeological collection at Pueblo Grande Museum. Research can be an exciting time of discovery, but also a lonely investigation. Staff at these institutions, under pressure of reductions, were all friendly and helpful. A special thanks to National Archives staff in Washington, D. C. and Laguna Niguel, California for their assistance in tracking down homesteading files and tract books.

The task of writing is rewarding; the compilation of the chapters, with integration of photos and maps, into a real book is challenging. Thanks to Mike Bercaw and his staff at Scottsdale's Sir Speedy for guiding my draft into a quality printed publication. And to Karen Friend who provided important skill in creating the maps and table. A heartfelt thanks to Bob Boze Bell and Leland Hanchett, Jr. for reviewing the manuscript.

Finally, thanks to my wife, Leslie, for her support and patience throughout. Even when I would wake up at 3 o'clock in the morning to jot down another purported brainstorm.

I hope you, the reader, enjoy this journey back to the pioneering days of frontier Phoenix.

CHAPTER ONE
Out of the Ruins

It was early December, 1867. Seventeen hardened pioneers, all men, most of whom were miners, gathered in Wickenburg along the Hassayampa River to embark upon a journey over to the Salt River. Their wagon and eight-mule team was loaded with tools and provisions. The group had a two-day journey ahead of them. This was the Swilling Party, led by the ever-restless seeker of fortune, Arizona pioneer Jack Swilling. Their objective - establish farms along the Salt River to supply wheat and other grains to military posts and mining camps.

To do this, the Swilling Irrigating and Canal Company had been formed earlier in mid-November in Wickenburg, with water claims filed in Prescott. The organizers consisted of Swilling, Fred Henry, Darrell Duppa, Thomas McGoldrick, Henry Wickenburg of Vulture Mine fame, Joseph Davis and Charles Clusker. In addition to their mining interests, Swilling and Wickenburg owned neighboring farms on the Hassayampa River. Other members included Gordon Wilson, James McCullen, Samuel Hensley, Frank Chapman (President) and Aaron Barnett (Treasurer). Capital stock of $10,000 was divided into 50 shares. Members unable to pay for shares could work for their share. Reportedly, most of the capital was provided by Wickenburg and Louis Jaeger, a successful Yuma ferryman. They claimed "all waters of Salt River or as much thereof as may be necessary, for milling, mining, farming and irrigating purposes." Swilling clearly had prior knowledge of the area for the claim referred to an "ancient acequia," "Buttes" (on the south side of the river at the future site of Tempe), and a "Hay Camp," referring to the wild grass farming efforts of John Smith

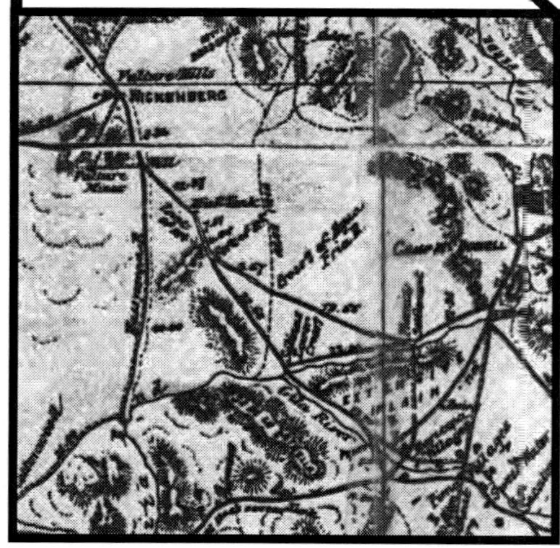

in the spring of 1867 (on land now occupied by the Phoenix International Airport).

Early explorers of the Salt River Valley, including Jack Swilling in his travels with the Walker Party in 1862-1863, used the Hassayampa River as their trail route heading southeastward to the Salt River. However, this was a treacherous journey through some rough and rocky terrain and not the most direct route. The Swilling Party likely followed the Hassayampa River to the general vicinity of where Smith's Mill was later located, then would have veered off across the desert on the recently-completed military trail to Fort McDowell. Water buckets were likely lashed to the side of the wagon as water would not be available until the crossing of the Agua Fria River. As dusk arrived, the Swilling Party would have stopped here (as settlement and trade increased, an actual stage station would be located in the vicinity of this crossing by 1871, somewhere between today's Bell Road and Grand Avenue). They would have slept under the stars in the crisp December air.

The Swilling Party set off in the morning, arriving at the Salt River a number of hours later. What might they have seen? The first European to visit the Salt River Valley was James Ohio Pattie, a fur trapper of the Southwest, in 1826. Following a fierce battle with the "Papawars," his party trapped for beaver in what he called at that time the Black River - "It [today's Salt River] affords as much water at this point as the Helay [Gila River] ... We found it to abound with beavers. It is a most beautiful stream, bounded on each side with high and rich bottoms."

In 1854, the John R. Bartlett survey party reached the Salt River on July 3. "The river we found to be from 80-120 feet wide, from two to three feet deep, and both rapid and clear ... The water is perfectly sweet, and neither brackish nor salt, as would be inferred from the name. We saw from the banks many fish in its clear waters and caught several of the same species as those taken in the Gila ... Along the immediate margin of the stream large cotton-wood trees grow."

In a more contemporary report, General James Rusling described his trip to the area in the spring of 1867: "and soon strike a huge acequia winding up from the Salt, in comparison with which all the acequias we had yet seen in Utah or California were the veriest ditches. It must be, I should think, thirty feet wide by ten or twelve feet deep, and seems like a great canal of modern times [the Montezuma ditch used by Mormon colonizers in 1877] ... So, there are other ancient acequias, furrowing the bottoms of the Salt on either side, though we observed none so large as this ... One thing is certain, these ancient builders -Aztecs or whoever they were - were at least good architects and engineers, and they must have peopled much of Arizona with an industrious and dense population."

Rusling went on to speculate that the river "must have been a larger river than it is now, or probably ever will be again; because two or three of these old acequias would carry off all its present waters, and leave none for the others, whose remains yet furrow the country there everywhere ... there are fine lands all along the bottoms of the Salt, and enough water flowing there yet to irrigate many thousands of acres. Indeed the best lands we saw in Arizona are here in the heart of it, on the Gila and Salt, and in time no doubt there will be flourishing settlement there."

William Pierce conducted a land survey in early 1867 on behalf of the U. S. Government to establish township and section boundaries. He was less concerned with archaeology and more with farming potential. He wrote that the soil along the Salt River "could be classed as first-rate composed of a sandy loam light, rich and easily worked ... The surface is generally level sloping gradually toward the north. Vegetation - mesquite and greasewood brush and in some places grass ... Salt River is at this season of the year at least a very large stream. Nor do I think it ever entirely dry. It has moreover a very heavy fall of I should think 12 to 15 ft to the mile which renders it especially valuable for irrigation. I consider this valley from 6 to 10 miles wide and extending from its mouth upward to the mountains about forty miles - as some of the best agricultural land I have yet seen in the Territory and would recommend that it be subdivided at an early day."

Wilfred Ingalls continued the federal survey work in March through July of 1868, noting more of the vegetation, particularly the cottonwood and willow trees along the river banks. Ingalls observed the mesquite as well as paloverde, greasewood and sagebrush. He reported that the Salt River provided fish for Indians. The mountains were "distinct and blue, like a grand picture." Correspondence to the *Arizona Miner* earlier that year characterized the valley as "rich and fertile." It was noted that "The River here is quite large ... and has lots of good fish, with plenty of ducks, geese, beaver and other game along the stream."

The Swilling Party certainly must have been captivated by this desert landscape, stretching in all directions as far as the eye could see. However, their goal was not to enjoy the beauty of the Salt River and its environs, but rather to control it. Water was viewed like a mining claim, a resource to be extracted and turned into a profitable product - in this case, an irrigation ditch that would ultimately produce valuable crops. They began their venture on the north bank of the river, across from the "Buttes." This site proved laden with rock-infused caliche; too much work for their mining picks and axes. Three miles downstream were the remains of a prehistoric Hohokam canal, perhaps dating back more than one thousand years (near the present-day Pueblo Grande Museum site). It was here, without fanfare but much backbreaking toil, that the Swilling Party picked and shoveled, completing the first portion of the Swilling Ditch on March 12, 1868. The canal era had begun.

A letter to Prescott's *Arizona Miner* (the only newspaper serving this wider area of Prescott, Wickenburg and the Salt River) reported in January of 1868 that "The above place, perhaps, is new to you, and to many readers of the *Miner*, not withstanding, it is settled principally by old Arizona pioneers, who do not intend it to remain a stranger long as it will certainly be one of the most important settlements in Arizona, and like the bird it derives it name from [Phoenix] will rise like smoke from a tar-kiln."

The story of the phoenix, the mythical bird with bright and colorful plumage, could be found in many cultures around the world. The story revolved around death and rebirth. The 500 year-old, dying phoenix was set on fire by the rays of the sun; yet, out of the ashes of that fire emerged a newborn phoenix. Appropriately for the Salt River Valley, the phoenix was associated in some cultures with the worship of the sun. The phoenix was also a popular symbol in early Christian art and literature, symbolizing Christ's death and resurrection.

Debate continues over who in the Swilling Party actually named this young community. The generally accepted story that came down anecdotally from other pioneers of that early period was later reported in the press in the 1880s. The story goes that Jack Swilling, one of the Starar brothers, Darrell Duppa and John Larsen were sitting around the camp one evening after a full day of working on the canal and wondered aloud about a name for the new settlement. Swilling apparently proposed it be named Stonewall, after General Stonewall Jackson of the Confederacy. That idea received no support. Starar suggested "Salina," an early recorded name for the Salt River. Others objected, not wishing to give outsiders the impression that there were salt marshes or a river bed of alkaline. Darrell Duppa, taking note of the extensive ruins of the area, suggested the name of Phoenix. His familiarity with the classics made him think of the phoenix, a mythical bird that rose out of the ashes to be reborn, just as a new civilization would rise out of the ruins of old. The words vary from author to author in various recollections. Most importantly, Phoenix became the accepted name and the Duppa legend was born.

Darrell Duppa, educated in Europe, was by far the most highly educated of the group and is indeed the most likely choice, as he is also given credit for naming Tempe. While Jack Swilling owned a dictionary, it is hard to picture the hardened frontiersman leafing though its pages over the light of the fire looking for a suitable name. The image of Phoenix, both the bird and the town, rising out of the ashes, or ruins of the Hohokam civilization, remains compelling.

Who were these men of the Swilling Party, these founders of the early Salt River settlement, known as Phoenix? Here is the list of names of these intrepid pioneers:

Peters Burns, Frank Chapman, Darrell Duppa, Jacob Denslinger, Thomas Hogue, James Lee, John Larson, Thomas McGoldrick, Michael McGrath, Thomas McWilliams, Frank Metzler, Antonio Moreas, James Smith, Jack Swilling, Ludvic Vandemark, Jack Walters, and Joseph Woods.

Several of these members did not remain long - Burns, Chapman, McGrath and Moreas - and are generally lost to recorded history. Several likely went back to mining, which is what James Lee was doing in 1880 in the Prescott area. James Smith was responsible for the first killing in the settlement in 1869 of a James Nelson and quickly departed the region, reportedly later seen with a band of Apaches.

McWilliams was known to have moved to Gila Bend, later operated a stage station on the Hassayampa River, and finally to have died near Fort Goodwin along the Gila River.

Others continued to farm for a time. Duppa, Larson, Metzler, Swilling, Vandemark, Walters and Woods all filed pre-emption land claims for their 160-acre farms. Thomas Hoague, who farmed for several years, inexplicably did not file. Only Duppa, Walters, and Vandemark show historical evidence of actually securing their homestead patents. Property records show that McGoldrick, Larson and Swilling sold their land in the early 1870s, as did Duppa and Vandemark. By the 1880 Census, only Jack Walters and Darrell Duppa remained in Phoenix. None of these early settlers participated in a leadership capacity in the new Phoenix Townsite, created in the 1870-1871 period. Jack Walters passed away in 1909, at the age of 85, the last local survivor of the Swilling Party.

Two members of the Swilling Party played influential roles and warrant further biographical treatment - Darrell Duppa, for his role in naming the new settlement; and, of course, Jack Swilling, for his larger than life reputation and his role as founder of the new settlement.

Darrell Duppa

Darrell Duppa was born in France in 1832 of English parents. His life's journey is shrouded in mystery. Even his Arizona days are difficult to trace. He was listed as a miner in Prescott in the 1864 Arizona Territorial Census. Duppa (actually he signed his name, Brian P. D. Dupper in his homestead papers; most historians have used the Duppa spelling) was likely mining in the Wickenburg area at the time of the formation of the Swilling Party. He was actually the first enumerated resident in the 1870 Census for the "Phoenix Precinct," with his age listed as 36 and his occupation as "farmer." Newspaper reports later in 1870 and 1871 placed him at the Agua Fria Well or Station on the road to Wickenburg.

However, in his Pre-Emption Proof of July, 1872, his witnesses, David Shultes and Jonathon Brian, said they had known him since 1871 and that he had settled the land in 1870 and resided there ever since. He was reported to have cultivated 120 acres and "has set out shade trees and live [ocotillo] fence." Duppa paid his $200 for the 160 acres south of the Phoenix Townsite on July 30, 1872. He received his patent in 1873 and sold his land and dwelling to John B. Montgomery shortly thereafter. The Duppa/Montgomery house, currently in deplorable condition, is one of the last remaining adobe dwellings in Phoenix from the frontier era.

While clearly a well-educated man in the classics and apparently of some wealthy family (he is often referred to as a "remittance man," receiving a regular financial stipend from his family in England), Darrell Duppa was a man of stark contrasts. John Bourke, author of On the Border with Crook, found him to be one of the "queerest examples to be found in Arizona ... he was hospitable to a fault, and not afraid of man or devil. Three bullet wounds, received in three different fights with the Apaches, attested to his grit." However, the Agua Fria Station was "nothing but a ramada," with a single room with a "long, unpainted table of pine, which served for meals or gambling ... [To provide protection from the wind] strips of canvas or gunny-sacking were tacked on the inner side of the cactus branches." Bourke wondered why Duppa would choose to live in such a "forlorn spot ... the best I could get to my queries was that the Apaches had attacked him ... And after he had repulsed them he thought he would stay there merely to let them know he could do it." He likely abandoned the station with the major flood of 1873 and returned to Phoenix.

Mary Gray, wife of pioneer farmer, Columbus Gray, who arrived in the valley in 1868, remembered Duppa would go off into the mountains and "sometimes when he came back he didn't look like a human ... He was as rough a character as you would want to see." But then she related, he would shave, clean up, "bought a new suit" and brought her "Sonoran oranges" from Maricopa. Trinidad Swilling recollected that "Lord Dupper" never had a permanent home, but "he had lot of friends" and moved from place to place. In the 1880 Census, Darrell

Duppa identified himself as a miner. He was living on Washington Street with another miner and a blacksmith. That same year he was arrested on a drunk and disorderly charge. In his last few years, he was living with Dr. and Mrs. O. J. Thibodo, where he passed away on January 30, 1892.

Jack Swilling

Jack Swilling would not have struck his contemporaries as a town founder. He was a pioneer frontiersman always on the move, looking for the next opportunity to discover fortune, not one to settle down for long. He had married Mary Jane Gray in Alabama in 1852, only to abandon her and his child in a quest for gold. He was a miner in 1858 along the Gila River, east of Yuma; in 1860 in the Pinos Altos, near Silver City, New Mexico; and in 1863 along the Hassayampa River in the Weaver Mountains. Swilling was a soldier in the Civil War, first for the Confederacy, then for the Union side. He was also an Indian fighter, participating in the surrender of Mangas Colorado in 1863 and in the infamous massacre of Apaches at Bloody Tanks with King Woolsey in 1864. That same year, he married Trinidad Escalante (age 17) in Tucson. In 1867, Jack Swilling was a farmer, raising crops and a family along the Hassayampa River, near the Wickenburg and Brill farms. He was considered to be both generous and dangerous, particularly if he had been drinking. Jack Swilling was 37 years old.

Jack Swilling

Perhaps it was a combination of all these characteristics that contributed to his leadership of the Swilling Party - feared yet respected, attuned to his mining associates yet recognizing the market potential for agriculture in the Salt River Valley. Swilling oversaw the construction of this first Swilling Ditch. He organized several other canal ventures in Phoenix, Tempe and in the later Lehi/Mesa area. It was reported that in early 1868, Swilling had cultivated 100 acres with wheat, barley and corn. In the first Territorial election of the newly-created voting precinct of Phoenix, Swilling was appointed to serve as inspector. Voting took place at his house and Jack Swilling was elected as the first Justice of the Peace in the new settlement along the Salt River.

In fact, his home, known as "Dos Casas" (near present-day 36th Street and Washington), was nearly a castle, certainly the largest adobe structure in the valley during the frontier era. Measuring 59 feet by 80 feet, the home of Jack and Trinidad was the social center of early Phoenix. Elections were held there. The first Post Office was there. William Hancock opened a store next to it. The first Catholic Mass was held there. In the 1870 Census, the Swillings had two daughters and two Indian orphans living with them. A successful farmer and community builder, Jack Swilling seemed to have found his place in the Arizona Territory.

Then, in the heated competition to select a townsite for the Maricopa County seat, his associates and friends abandoned him. In that one stroke in the elections of May, 1871, when voters decided that the proposed townsite west of the Swilling Castle was preferable for the new County seat, Swilling's fortunes had changed. He reportedly shot a Mexican who had not voted his way. In July of 1871, he advertised his ranch for sale. In 1872, he was arraigned for assault to commit murder but found not guilty. This only added to his reputation for violence. An advertisement in the *Arizona Miner* in June of 1872 again offered his 160-acre ranch for sale, including 300 grape vines and a nine-room adobe house. Later that year, he joined with Governor Safford to organize a new canal on the Upper Gila and was reportedly preparing to move there near Camp Goodwin. This venture did not materialize. In 1873, William Hellings purchased the Swilling ranch for $3,000.

That same year Jack and Trinidad Swilling and their family moved into a small rock cabin on the east bank of the Agua Fria River near Black Canyon, just off the road to Phoenix. There he farmed, mined, raised cattle, and operated a stage station. In 1878, the family moved once more, this time to the mining town of Gillette. In the Spring, he and two friends, having boasted during a drinking spree about robbing a stage, were arrested. They were taken to the Yuma County jail.

In a revealing letter "To the Public" from jail, Swilling professed his innocence. His letter alluded to a broken skull suffered while in Texas and a bullet still carried in the left side of his body. "No one knows what I have suffered from these wounds ... At times they render me almost crazy ... During these periods of debauch, caused by the mixture of morphine and liquor [one historian has written that Swilling was addicted to Perry Davis Vegetable Pain Killer, an elixir containing both alcohol and opium], I have insulted my best friends ... I have gone to the rescue of my fellow men when they were surrounded by Indians - I have given to those who needed - I have furnished shelter to the sick. From the Governors down to the lowest Mexicans in the land have I extended my hospitality ... Oh God, is it possible that poor old Jack Swilling should be accused of such a crime? ... Brought on by crazy, drunken talk ... I may be found dead any morning in my cell ... And may God help my poor family through this cold world is my prayer." On August 12, 1878, still awaiting trial, Jack Swilling died in jail.

In spite of all of his accomplishments, the *Salt River Herald* carried only a one-line report from Yuma, "Jack Swilling died here last night in jail." The *Territorial Expositor* wrote that "He was in ill health when brought to this place and the confinement and heat added to his general prostration so that medical skill could not save him." The paper carried his prison letter on September 21, 1878. A month later, Jack Swilling and his friends were found innocent of the stage robbery.

Trinidad Swilling and family moved back to Phoenix, where some townspeople took up a collection for the family. She took in sewing to make ends meet and was able to sell several town lots. Trinidad remarried and had three sons. She died in 1925 at the age of 78. Together, she and her husband, Jack Swilling, can take significant credit for the founding and establishment of the first Anglo-Mexican settlement along the Salt River. While there is a Swilling Butte in the Grand Canyon and a Swilling Gulch near the ghost town of Gillette, no place name in Phoenix recognizes their historic contributions. His body rests somewhere in Yuma in an unmarked grave. An ignominious conclusion to a flawed but fearless and visionary Arizona pioneer and leader.

The Swilling settlement, later known briefly as Pumpkinville, then Mill City and then East Phoenix, grew from an all-male contingent. Several others followed Swilling from Wickenburg shortly after the digging expedition: Frenchy Sawyer, the Starar brothers, Aaron Barnett, and James Murphy, to name a few. Charles Adams and his family came up from Adamsville on the Gila. The Grays and Pattersons, along with Hosea Greenhaw, arrived late in 1868. Thomas Barnum arrived that year, as did John Alsap and William Osborn, the latter two from Prescott. Other early farmers included George Freeman, F. S. Johnson, and William Rowe - these latter three, however, were gone by 1870. Rowe and his family moved further up river along the Salt River, near the Camp McDowell crossing and future site of Lehi/Mesa.

1870, a short two years later, found a fledgling community of 240 people. The 1870 Census provides a revealing profile. The area was known by its post office name - Phoenix. The population was almost evenly split between Anglos and Mexicans. Not surprisingly, the vast majority of the heads of household were single males, 68 Anglos and 80 Mexicans. Nearly all were farmers or farm laborers. Three Anglo married men out of thirteen, including John Ammerman, Jack Swilling and John Averish, were married to women from Mexico. There were 22 households of two or more persons, with eight Anglo families with children and five Mexican families with children. Albeit small, there were now children in the settlement. The Phoenix population also included three blacks, Mary Green and her two children; Mary worked as a cook and servant for the Grays.

While settlers from Confederate states were evident in good numbers (42%), there was sizeable representation from northern states (31%) and the foreign-born (26%). In short, Phoenix represented a surprisingly diverse population for the Arizona Territory, more akin to the composition of Tucson than Prescott.

From a tiny settlement along the early canal ditches, there were 69 dwellings in 1870. Farmers living alone; farmers with their families; farmers with their laborers; a blacksmith with his laborer; a saloon keeper living with his partner behind the saloon; a merchant living alone; two stage drivers in the same dwelling. Except for the Swilling Castle, the preponderance of the early adobes were likely less than 400 square feet. Anglo heads of household accounted for 52 of those dwellings, while Mexicans occupied the other 17 dwellings.

From the founding Swilling Party in December of 1867 to August of 1870, Phoenix had now become a community attracting some notice. The *San Francisco Evening Bulletin* wrote that year - "On Salt River is a settlement of about 300 people engaged exclusively in agriculture ... Mr. Swilling, an intelligent farmer, is of the opinion that by carefully managing the water of this stream, the entire arable land of the valley could be brought under cultivation." These were prophetic words indeed.

CHAPTER TWO
Managing the Salt River

The story of the settlement of Phoenix is the story of the harnessing of the Salt River through canal development. It is the story of how early settlers used mining claim precedence and practice to claim and control the future of a major natural resource - the water of the Salt River. It is the story of fulfilling an almost unimaginable vision - the creation of an agricultural oasis in the middle of the Sonoran Desert.

The saga begins with the Hohokam experience. The prehistoric Hohokam were an agricultural people who settled in northern Mexico and what would become southcentral Arizona from approximately A.D. 1 to 1450. Their name is derived from the Pima Indian (Akimel O'odham) for "those who have gone" or "all used up." In the prehistoric Southwest, the Hohokam were the premier agricultural peoples. Fields were planted in the Salt River Valley between rows of lateral irrigation canals as well as along washes. One noted archaeologist has written, "Using simple tools, the Hohokam created the largest prehistoric irrigation system in North America." All of this was done by hand, without draft animals, using stones hoes, stone axes and digging sticks. Moreover, the Hohokam exercised a working knowledge of engineering and hydraulics in order to create the proper flow with the appropriate gradient of the land.

Built over several centuries, well over five hundred miles of canals emanated from several points in the Salt River, transmitting water to tens of thousands of acres of fields. The Hohokam constructed weirs of rock and brush out into the Salt River, serving as diversion dams. Headgates were built with vertical log posts, then filled with brush and interwoven with reeds. The largest recorded Hohokam canal covered nearly 20 miles. Canal sizes ranged from 30-50 feet in width, and with embankments, up to 20 feet deep. The Hohokam harvested fields of corn, beans and squash through means of these canals as well as by floodwater farming. They also nurtured the growth of wild desert plants such as agave and cholla cactus.

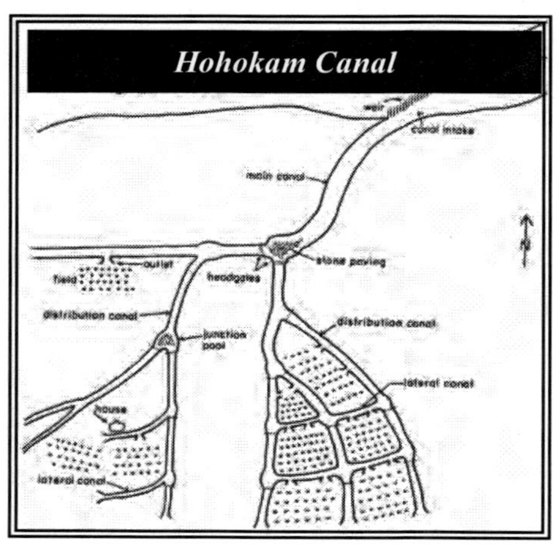

Hohokam Canal

Hohokam canals radiated throughout the Valley, leading to Hohokam villages like Pueblo Grande, La Ciudad and Los Colinas. It was the ruins of these villages and canals, suggesting a prosperous agricultural civilization, that prompted early Anglo visions of farming potential. Both James Rusling and Jack Swilling had seen this in 1867 in separate journeys. John Alsap would comment on it in 1872 - "That this whole Valley has at some time been densely populated cannot be doubted although neither history, tradition nor legend give any account of who the inhabitants were, from whence they came or whither they have gone. The whole Valley is dotted with the ruins of ancient towns and buildings. The great canal, commonly called the "Montezuma Acequia," intersects the river near the upper end of the Valley and runs thence in a northwesterly direction for several miles ... Smaller ditches leading out from it at convenient distances show that it was used for purposes of irrigation and the whole Valley has been under cultivation." Not surprisingly, Jack Swilling and other settlers dug the frontier canals in close proximity to Hohokam canal pathways.

Swilling's Canal, about two and one-half miles in length (beginning just west of today's Pueblo Grande Museum) was soon joined by the Davis Ditch. Ingalls survey of 1868 showed two ditches and several dwellings and two major fields. The size of the fields were probably understated, for an April 18, 1868 letter to the *Arizona Weekly Miner* identified nearly 700 acres of land under cultivation by the following farmers: Swilling, Freeman, Burns, Hoague, Duppa, Vandermark, Adams, Sawyer, Rowe, Johnson and Davis. It did not mention Denslinger, McGoldrick, Larsen and Walters who were also farming at the time and were members of the original Swilling Party.

The canal craze had begun. Claims were taken out all along the Salt River. The Arizona territorial law, known as the Howell Code, adopted in 1864, provided for the use of Arizona's water resources: "all streams, lakes, and ponds of water capable of being used for the purposes of navigation or irrigation are hereby declared to be public property, and no individual or corporation shall have to right to appropriate

Ingall's 1868 Survey

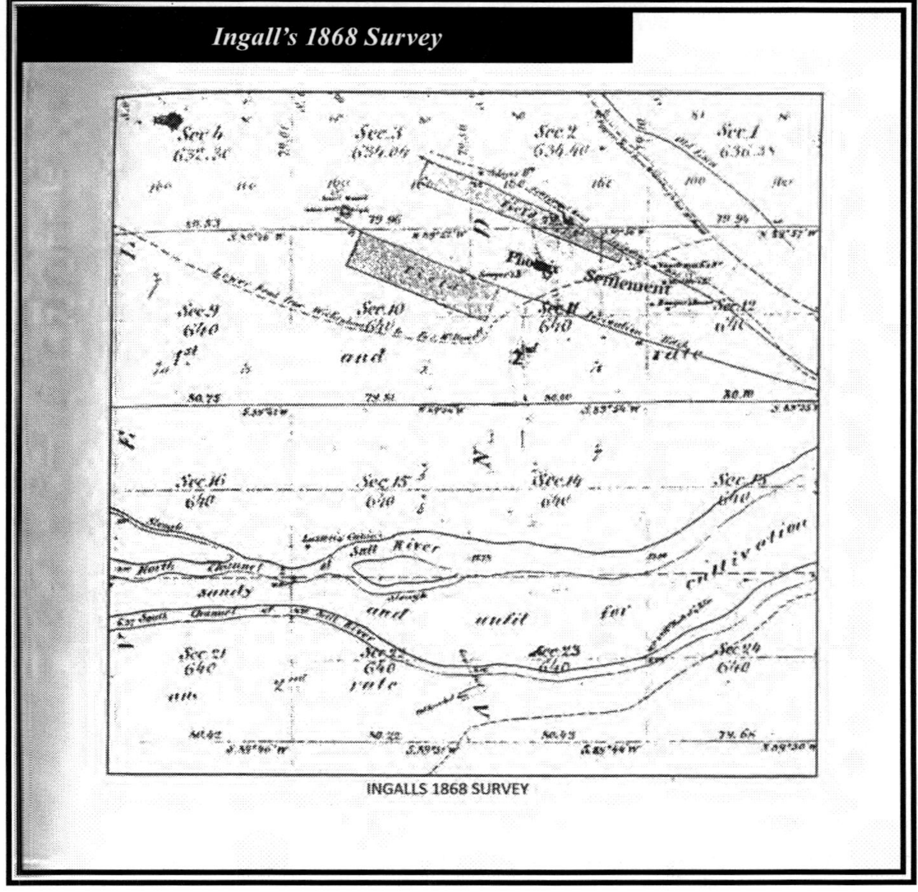

INGALLS 1868 SURVEY

Turney Map

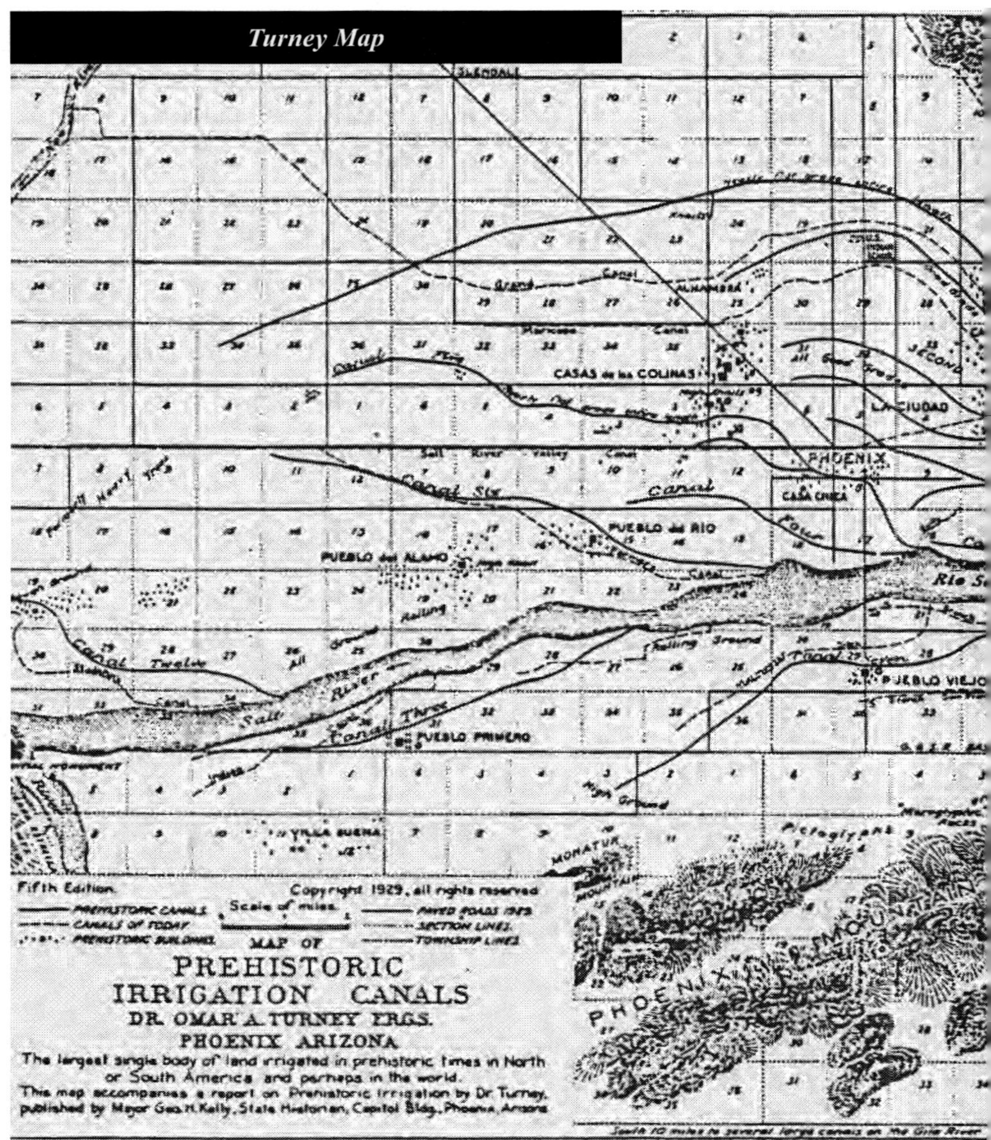

them exclusively to their own private use." Other sections of the Code allowed for both public and private canals. Priority was given to the oldest water rights in times of scarcity.

The Turney Map and the following list of canals depict the numerous claims and ditches taken out on both sides of the Salt River, both

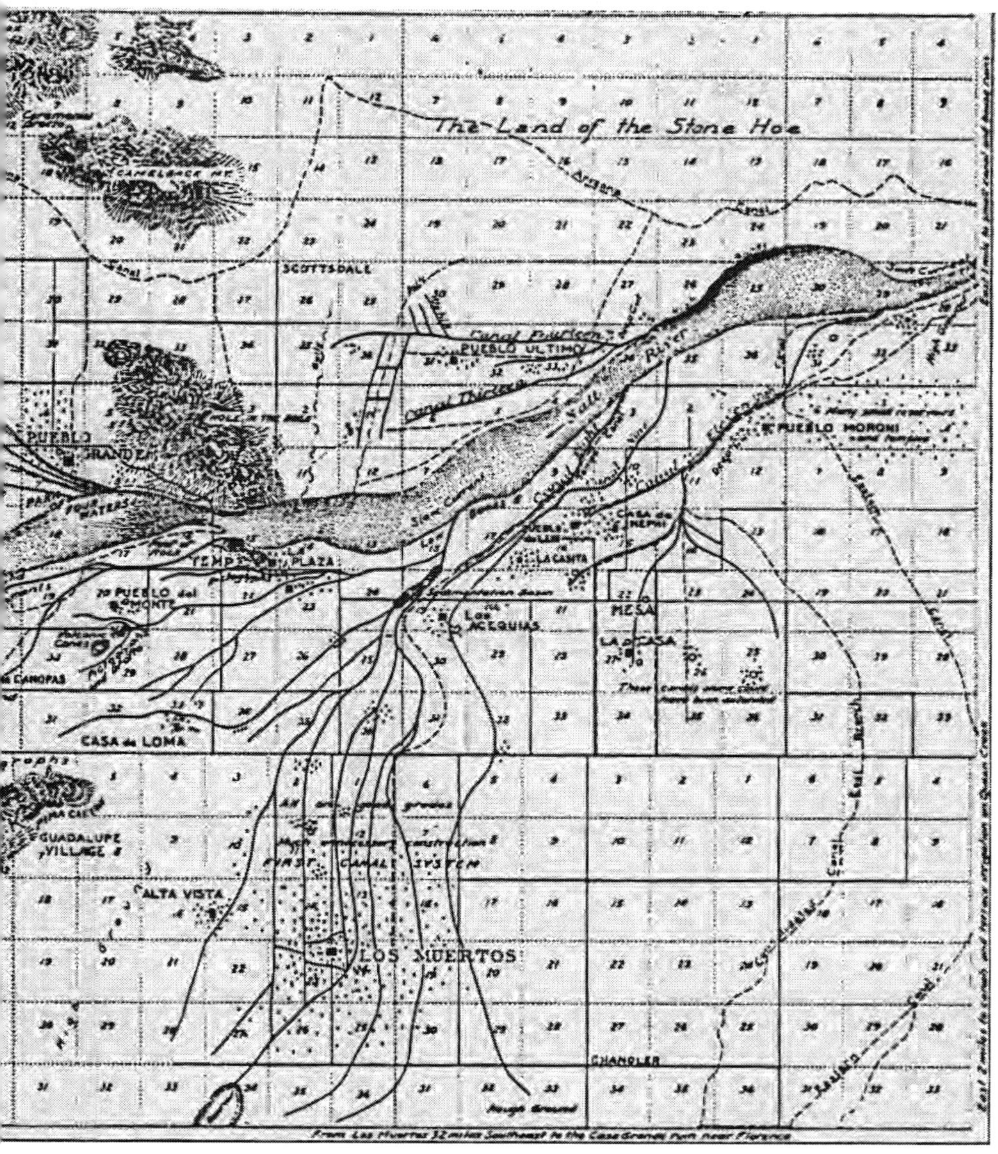

in prehistoric times and in early Phoenix: Swilling, Wilson, Dutch Ditch, Juan Chivri or later Griffin, Salt River Valley, Maricopa and the Monterey Ditch serving farmers to the north; and the Mexican (later San Francisco), Prescott, Virginia, Van Arman and Maddox, the Enterprise, and Watson (little is known about the last three) served south and southwest farmers. Canals were built by Anglo and

Mexican labor. Within four years at least 15 canals of varying length served the Phoenix community.

The largest of these was the Swilling Ditch, developed over time into three branches, and claiming 12,000 miners' inches of water. One, the Extension, became known as the Town Ditch, running west along Van Buren, eventually to a length of 19 miles at a width of about 20 feet. The North Extension became known as the Maricopa Canal and, by the late 1890s, was 26 miles in length. The Dutch Ditch ran only five miles. In 1875, the original Swilling Irrigating and Canal Company was dissolved and reorganized into the Salt River Valley Canal Company and the Maricopa Canal Company. John Alsap was the Secretary to both companies. Columbus Gray and William Hancock were incorporators of both. William Hellings, of Hellings Mill, owned shares in each company.

In 1878, the Grand Canal was constructed to provide water to west valley farmers. It was the first corporate canal (others being mutual associations), with an eventual length of 25 miles. William Hancock was the company's secretary and treasurer. The Cartwright farms were important beneficiaries. They and others built the canal. Jasper Cartwright described the ditch system on his land in his homesteading

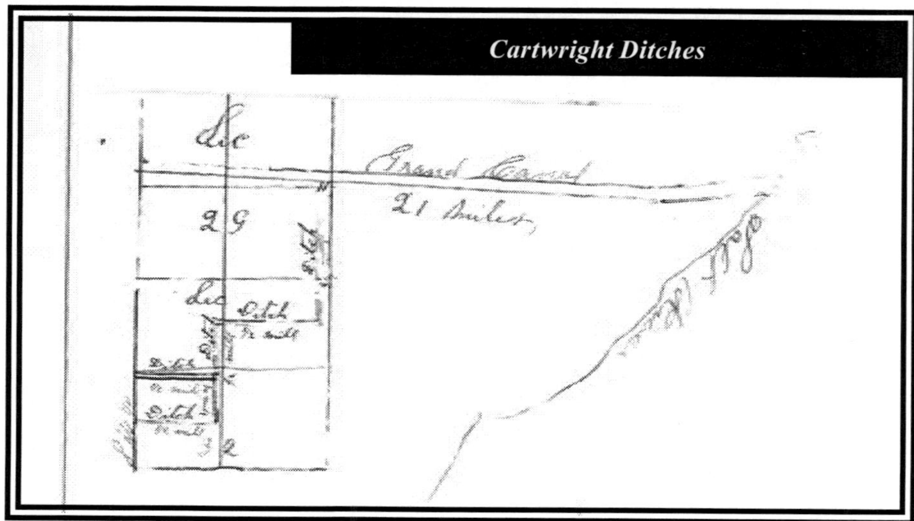

Cartwright Ditches

filing - "The land was flooded [from December to May by the Grand Canal]. The width five feet. Average depth 15 inches. There are two ditch, one running on the north side of the tract. The other through the center. Both run from east to west and each ditch is one-half mile long. There is another ditch [illegible] ¼ mile long connecting other two ditches." Neighboring farmer, William Issac, stated that the Cartwrights had about 80 acres in wheat, yielding about 1700 pounds to the acre.

Around the same time period, William Hancock built an extension from the Grand Canal: "I was obliged to construct this ditch for a length of ten miles" to reach his 640-acre farm even further west (current City of Avondale). His homesteading file, associated with his Desert Land Act filing, provided documentation of the value of irrigation. His witnesses to his Homesteading Proof wrote that "said land is barren and entirely devoid of vegetation except occasional sage brush, greasewood and scrub mesquite and that no crops have ever been raised upon similar land except by irrigation ... that no portion of said land will produce any agricultural crop of any description without irrigation." While no crops had yet been planted, in his deposition to his Proof, Hancock indicated he owned shares in the Grand Canal.

The physical construction of all these canals was quite similar to that of the Hohokam. The first step, following the location in the Salt River, was to build a diversion dam, out of brush and river rock. This directed the flow of the water to the entrance of the actual canal through a spillway. The spillway allowed the water to return to the river in the event of a flood to prevent or minimize damage to the headgate. The headgate was used to control the amount of water that went into the system. In the early years, canals were likely dug with axes and shovels by hand and later with scrapers pulled by draft animals. Grand Canal construction even employed dynamite.

The canals were cooperative ventures of adjoining farmers, by and large. However, given that water shares could be purchased and sold, there was an undetermined level of speculation in canal stock, as well.

Shareholders shared in the cost of construction, maintenance and repair, often with the farmers supplying their own labor.

Water distribution was managed by an overseer, often called the "zanjero," employed by the canal company. These zanjeros oversaw repair work, collected assessments and managed the proper distribution of water to individual farms. Each farmer also had a headgate and a water measuring box, designed to measure the number of inches of water permitted for that farm. Even the Phoenix Townsite had a zanjero, employed by the Town Association. Thomas Childs, a jailer and later candidate for City Marshal, was paid $11.66 for 21 days of work in early 1876. By March of that year, he was succeeded by David Moore, who received a monthly salary of ten dollars.

Similar to events during the Hohokam period, flooding was a concern to the proper year-round functioning of the canal system. The floods of January, 1874 and again in 1875, presented a challenge. As the *Arizona Miner* reported, "All parts of the valley flooded and people left homes and came to town." Headgates and diversions dams were washed away. Sand filled canal bottoms. The original headgate of the Swilling Ditch was likely abandoned at this time. Monsoon season in July and August was a constant threat. A young Mormon pioneer girl wrote in 1878 that "We [in Mesa] have had such terrible rains that it has kept the men busy watching and fixing breaks. It rained for nearly two weeks off and on ... I never saw rain come down so fast. It literally poured. Every little gulch and ravine was running streams."

At the end of the frontier era, it is estimated that water claims exceeded more than five times the river's annual flow. Eleven canal companies operated on each side of the Salt River throughout the Valley, in addition to smaller, independently-owned ditches. Discussions of a larger, unified cooperative plan for managing water had failed, despite the flooding incidents and conversely, times of low river flow. The Salt River was not yet tamed. In the meantime, these early canals were indeed the catalyst for a growing agricultural community. More and more farming homesteads were settled along and towards the terminus of each canal. As early as 1868, the *Arizona Miner* reported that "wheat and barley had all been harvested and shipped to Wickenburg where it has been sold at eight cents per pound." In 1871, the Territorial Legislature authorized the development of a promotional booklet on the "Resources of the Arizona Territory," published in San Francisco. It was written for persons "desiring to emigrate to this Territory." Referring to the Salt River Valley, the report noted that "there is an abundance of water in Salt River for the use of a vast extent of country ... There are thousands of acres of excellent land in this valley yet unoccupied that can be pre-empted and purchased by actual settlers for $1.25 per acre."

A paper written by John T. Alsap, "Resources of the Salt River Valley, 1872" provided a detailed accounting of both canals and farming at that time. "In 1870, about 2,000 acres of land was cultivated [generally on 160-acre farms] and at this time 5,000 acres are under cultivation and the settlement has a population of about 700 ... And now [Phoenix] bids fair to be a flourishing town." He went on to postulate that "About 50,000 acres of land in this great valley is known to be good for grain growing and double that amount is supposed to be [open to cultivation]. All that is necessary is that water be brought to it for irrigation. Nothing can be raised here without irrigation and with it almost any kind of crop can be raised ... Several ditches are in process of construction and will be completed this season in time for a corn crop."

"The principal crops are barley, wheat, corn, sorghum, Irish potatoes, sweet potatoes and peanuts [principally barley and wheat]. Cotton and tobacco have also been tried successfully but not to any great extent while almost any known garden vegetable can be raised in abundance. The average yield per acre of wheat, barley and corn is about 2,000 lb. per acre. The average price of grain last year was 4 ½ cts per pound and all that was raised found ready sale. At present grain is worth 5 ½ cts per pound. No tame hay has been cut here to my knowledge but alfalfa does well and I think clover would be a good crop. Sorghum and corn fodder is the principal rough feed for stock and sells for about $10.00 per ton."

"But few experiments in the way of fruit raising have been tried in the valley but in every instance, when tried, have proved successful. This season a large number of fruit trees of almost every kind have been put out and I have no doubt will prove profitable ... The low mountains skirting the valley are covered with excellent grasses and would be good stock range were it not for the danger from the Indians ... Labor on a farm is worth about $35 per month or $1.50 per day with board ... ."

"Most of the goods and groceries used in this region are brought from San Francisco either by water to Ft. Yuma and thence about 200 miles by land, or overland from Los Angeles 500 miles. Owing to the great length of time usually required to freight by water to Ft. Yuma the greater portion of the goods brought here is freighted overland from Los Angeles at a cost of about 12 cts per pound ... ."

"It is a very simple process to get a farm in this vicinity. A man settles on a quarter section and that is as good a title as need want for the present. The lands are all surveyed and preempted of which privilege some have availed themselves. But in order to make a farm productive a man must have water for irrigation on it and the getting of water to his land, the ditches generally, is the largest cost of his farm. But once the water is there he has a sure thing for a crop. Dry weather does not affect him -- he makes it rain on his farm whenever he pleases. Improved farms rate at from $1,000 to $6,000 in this valley."

Alsap's insightful, first-hand knowledge is an invaluable portrait of the agricultural area of Phoenix. He recognized the lack of farm machinery in that time period - "There is great want of agricultural machines also. We have not a mower, reaper or header for harvesting our crops nor is there a gang plow or seed sower in the valley." At the outset, farming was done by hand, with a crooked stick plow for plowing. Then, headers came into use, clipping the heads of the grain from the stalk. The first threshers were brought into the valley by two farmers from Wickenburg and Florence. Alsap noted that by 1872 several local farmers had their own threshers that were rented out for use to other farms. This transaction occurred on a "royalty" basis, one-twelfth of the grain threshed going to the thresher with the balance to the farm that also furnished the labor to bring the grain to the machine. It was estimated that it cost $10 per acre to cut and thresh grain and prepare it for market in the early 1870s.

The Mormon colonizers quickly recognized the agricultural possibilities upon entering the Valley in 1877. "Wheat sown in winter can be cut in May, after which the land can be plowed, watered, and corn planted, thus producing two crops of different kinds ... The topsoil is fine, sandy loam with an underlayer of clay; making a splendid mixture for wheat when broken up," reported one pioneer. All of the early farmers learned which crops grew best during which season and exercised constant vigilance to regulate the quantity and timing of water from the ditches throughout the two growing seasons. Winter wheat, barley, some vegetables and a few other crops were harvested during the winter months, while most grasses, corn, sorghum, fruits and vegetables were reaped from spring until fall.

Harvesting, therefore, was a full-time job in the hot summer months of the Sonoran Desert. A Mormon pioneer described this hands-on process: "Before they [farmers] had threshing machines they would hire Mexicans to cut the grain with sickles. They would pile it in piles then haul it in. They would prepare a place -- set a tall pole in the middle of a circle of hard clean ground, then put the grain all around this circle then tie a long rope to this pole, then tie six or seven horses side by side to this rope. Someone would get on a horse behind them and keep the horses going until the grain was all out of the heads. When there was a good breeze blowing, they would take a pitch fork and pitch it in the air. All of the coarse straw would blow out. Then we would run it through a little fanning machine we turned by hand. This is the way the Indians always threshed their grain only they would use baskets which they had made instead of a fanning machine."

Charles Crismon, a Mormon farmer, described his day as a younger man, at harvest time: "I cut all the hay -- cut it and bucked it to the stack. I would get up early, milk the two cows, grind my knives on the grinding stone, (I had to tread it with my feet) and harness the horses ... I would be in the field by sunup and work until sundown for $1.50 per day. By the time I got supper over with and milked two cows it was bedtime."

Harvest time during the summer months was quite a daunting task. Another Mormon pioneer wrote that "It is not so hot but men of pluck and energy work at harvesting or thrashing 14 hours per day [sometimes] working 16 men and 22 horses. They lift the grain on the tables with derrick forks. Have had only to lay off two weeks on account of rain. They board their hands at the stack ... and thresh from 20,000 to 50,000 pounds of grain per day." Another farmer recalled, "As summer advanced, I often saturated my clothing with water before starting to hoe a row of corn forty rods long, and before reaching the end, my clothes were entirely dry."

In a good growing season under good harvesting conditions, a threshing crew working for two or more months could potentially harvest an enormous amount of grain. Since mechanical threshers, and the tools and machinery used with them, were very expensive, most farmers rented or shared the services of these machines during harvest time. This type of cooperation kept their labor and equipment costs down in order to improve their chances of a good return on grain at market and plenty of surplus for their own use.

Critical to the success of early agriculture was the establishment of a milling operation in the area. Early Phoenix Townsite leaders recognized this with the outright donation of an entire block to William Bichard (who operated a similar mill in Adamsville). However, his mill burned down in September of 1871, after only four months of operation. The enterprising William Hellings was more successful with his steam-powered flour mill, located north of the Swilling Ranch, along the same canal. In the fall of 1871, Hellings had his mill machinery shipped by boat from San Francisco to Ehrenburg on the Colorado River and then freighted overland to the Valley by the Miller brothers of Prescott.

One correspondent came to the Hellings' property in 1872-73 and gave the following account: "It had the appearance of a poor Mexican settlement; a few adobe houses, with the mill owned by the Helling (sic) Brothers, standing out like an imposing monument. The Helling brothers with Mr. Wm. Hancock, Mr. John Y. T. Smith and Mr. ---Evans were the principal residents."

"Mr. Helling and his brother lived in a one story adobe well fitted up with comfortable furniture and we can well remember the pleasant room with a bright, new carpet covering the mud floor, the pictures on the walls, curtains at the windows, the long narrow hall through the center of the house, with the hanging olla with cool water ... But there was one luxury Mr. Helling did indulge in - a good Chinaman cook ... Later on beds were placed in this hall for the men of our party; the women occupying the furnished rooms."

By 1875, the Hellings mill not only milled grain for surrounding farmers but their enterprise was also making pork, bacon and lard from a hog-raising venture. That same year, he opened a store in Tucson. Hinton's Handbook to Arizona, published in 1878, described the East Phoenix settlement as a "very pretty little hamlet gathered about a large flouring mill, with water running on either side of its only street, which for half a mile is also lined with young cottonwood trees." By this time, Hellings mill, was now known as the Salt River Flouring Mill, and owned and operated by Charles Veil, one of Hellings' former partners. In the Phoenix Townsite, John Y. T. Smith and King Woolsey had opened the Phoenix Flour Mill, while across the river in Tempe, Charles Hayden operated the only water-powered mill.

In its inaugural issue of January of 1878, the *Salt River Herald* reported, somewhat lyrically, that " the soil is well adapted to the prosperous growth of all cereals, barley and wheat being at present the principal crops ... Wherever the irrigation system can be made to reach the plant, the farmer has only to tickle the earth with the hoe and it laughs with a harvest, unrivalled in its range and profusion."

At the end of the decade, the Disturnall Arizona Business Directory provided this description of agriculture in the Salt River Valley by P. Hamilton, Territorial Statistician: "After a drive through its immense fields of golden grain, ripening in the early summer sun, one is impressed with the almost unlimited capabilities of this valley, which has been well named the 'Garden of the Territory'. No one who has not visited the Salt River country can have any conception of the area of land which has been reclaimed for the desert, brought under a high state of cultivation, and made fruitful and highly productive. For nearly thirty miles up and down the course of the river there is almost one continuous line of fine farms, bearing bountiful crops. A ride through this grand grain field is a sight the like of which is found nowhere else in the Territory. Wheat and barley are the principal crops, but immense stretches of alfalfa, beautiful with its bluish purple blossoms, and waving gently in the summer breeze, like an emerald lake, greet the eye in every direction. Comfortable farm-houses, embowered in groves of cottonwood and poplar, and acequias, lined with shade trees, most admirably diversify the landscape; while the rugged mountains, their outlines softened in a purple haze, complete the picture of this Arizona Arcadia, whose semi-tropical loveliness is the glory of our Territory."

"It is estimated that there are over 15,000 acres of land under cultivation in the valley at the present time, more than half of which is in wheat. The average yield is about fifteen hundred pounds to the acre. The wheat crop for the present year presents a splendid appearance, and will compare with that of any section of the Pacific Coast. The barley crop is now being harvested, as I passed through the valley large number of farm hands with threshers and headers, were scattered in every direction, gathering the ripened grain ... The sickle and scythe have given place to the header and its labor-saving appurtenances. The farmers of Salt River ... use the latest and most perfect agricultural machinery, and the work of gathering the crop is done cheaply and expeditiously. Leading farmers have informed your correspondent that they can raise grain in this valley as cheaply as in California."

Early Valley pioneers were enticed to farming by virtue of this potential and the irrigation canals of the Salt River. Neither farmer nor policy maker in the Arizona Territory were discouraged by the knowledge of limited rainfall in the arid West. In fact, they were more likely aware of and encouraged by spurious science and the quixotic optimism that "Rain Follows the Plow."

This theory was advanced by Josiah Gregg's widely-read book, Commerce of the Prairies, published in 1844 - "The high plains seem too dry and lifeless ... Why may we not suppose that the genial influences of civilization - that extensive cultivation of the earth - might contribute to the multiplication of showers, as it certainly does of fountains? Or that shady groves, as they advance upon the prairies may have some effect upon the seasons?" Even the eminent geographer, Ferdinand Haydn, postulated "that the planting of ten or fifteen acres of forest trees on each quarter section [160 acres] will have a most important effect on the climate, equalizing and increasing the moisture and adding greatly to the fertility of the soil."

The Commissioner of the General Land Office, the administrator of federal land policy such as the Homesteading Act, wrote in 1866: "If one-third of the surface of the Great Plains were covered with forest, there is every reason to believe the climate would be greatly enhanced, the greater portion of the soil would be susceptible to a high degree of cultivation." Richard Smith Elliott, who worked for the railroads and contributed to Haydn's reports in the early 1870s, not surprisingly contended that even the building of railroads increased rainfall. There was voluminous discussion and writings on "this bit of meteorological fantasy" during the 1860s and 1870s, including a report on the subject written by Elliott and published by the Smithsonian. All of this eventually led to the Timber Culture Act of 1873 and then the Desert Land Act of 1877, the latter formally requiring irrigation of otherwise desolate, virgin land.

Charles Dana Wilber, a speculative town builder and amateur scientist, wrote in 1881, what others had already come to believe - ... "on the sweat of his face, toiling with his hands, man can persuade the heavens to yield their treasures of dew and rain upon the land he has taken for his dwelling place ... The raindrop never fails to fall and answer the power of prayer and labor." Human settlement would increase rainfall and allow for the successful homesteading of what had previously only been known as the "Great American Desert."

Historian Henry Nash Smith could have been writing of the experience of frontier Phoenix when he wrote about the opening of the Western lands over the twenty years following the passage of the Homesteading Act in 1862: "the image of the garden in the West ... had triumphed over the image of the desert." The arrogant confidence of Manifest Destiny had triumphed over science. Even the editors of the *Salt River Herald*, writing in 1878, subscribed to this popular theory. It was reported that there had been more rain the past season and summer temperatures had been cooler, perhaps a relative term even for that time. They contended this was due to more tree plantings, ditches and cultivated acreage. "The history of other States and Territories all prove that with increased population and consequent improvement the climate has greatly changed. We are of the opinion that inside of five years owing to these changes the thermometer will never have occasion to go above the 95 degree mark." This did not happen.

A lone voice in the debates of that era was John Wesley Powell. The much-regaled explorer of the Colorado River had become an important national scientist. In his document, entitled "A Report on the Lands of the Arid Region of the United States," published in 1876, Powell wrote, "if it be true that increase of the water supply is due to increase in precipitation, as many have supposed, the fact is not cheering to the agriculturalist of the arid region ... Any great change [in climate] is ephemeral, and usually changes go in cycles, and the opposite or compensating change may reasonably be anticipated ... [We] shall have to expect a speedy return to extreme aridity, in which case a large portion of the agricultural industries of these now growing up would be destroyed." His rather circuitous debunking of "the rain follows the plow" myth upset both Western boosters and politicians.

But, while Powell's treatise on the West has sometimes been viewed as anti-development, he was simply promoting a more rational and cautious settlement, water and agriculture policy. Powell challenged both the 160-acre farm as well as the sacrosanct nature of riparian rights. His solution was neither more land nor more irrigation but rather a revolutionary and more efficient unified water system predicated on regional solutions, incorporating both dams and on-stream reservoirs. Requiring more capital and cooperation than could be realized at the local level, as had been witnessed during this same time period with halting water discussions in the Salt River Valley, Powell recognized the federal government would have to intervene to superimpose a water and irrigation solution for the larger community.

John Wesley Powell's ideas and vision fell on deaf ears in the 1870s and 1880s. No state wanted to be even referred to publicly as "arid;" that deflated the boosterism of the day. A federal role was anathema to the political dogma of most Western states. His miscalculation of potential support for his scientific perspective cost him dearly in both public and political circles.

In hindsight, Powell was prophetic. He was well aware of the importance of proper irrigation to ensure agricultural growth and settlement, a fact not lost on early Phoenix pioneers. And he was certainly aware of the struggles individual regions encountered with haphazard and fragmented water systems. At the time, regions like the Salt River Valley were simply inclined to work through water issues on a seasonal basis; no one vision or group of leaders were capable of creating an acceptable solution. It would be left to a succeeding generation of Salt River Valley leaders to successfully adopt a regional water supply plan to advance a more sustainable, agricultural-based future.

Powell's call for federal intervention would one day be heeded. In fact, the legislative foundation of large-scale federal dam and irrigation projects, the National Reclamation Act of 1902, was passed shortly after Powell's death. As Marc Reisner wrote in <u>Cadillac Desert</u>, the 20th century witnessed a "rampage" of "dam-building and irrigation development which, in all probability, went far beyond anything Powell would have liked."

CHAPTER THREE
Claiming the Desert

Homesteading. It conjures up the notion of free land. It calls to mind the sod house novels of Laura Ingalls Wilder. Or the Oklahoma land rush. Generous federal land policies fueled western settlement in the mid-nineteenth century. Early settlers in the Salt River Valley during the 1870s were well aware of their options in procuring land. When the Ingalls survey work was approved, the Prescott Land Office opened its doors for new homestead claims in the desert of the Salt River Valley in December of 1870.

The filing response was swift and significant. Within ten days, 30 filings had occurred in the four townships around the early canals. Those first settlers claimed early - Jack Swilling, the Elliott brothers, the Bucks, John Larson, Columbus Gray, William Hellings, John Alsap, William Osborn, Hosea Greenhaw, Gordon Wilson. 50 more were filed in 1871; another 42 in 1872. Nearly all of these claims were for 160 acres. And each of them had to travel to the Prescott Land Office to secure these claims.

In the early filings, homesteaders could apply under the Pre-Emption Act of 1841 or the National Homestead Act of 1862. The former legislation was yet another attempt, dating back over sixty years, to somehow accommodate those who claimed public land in anticipation of future federal surveys and land sales. President Tyler called a special session of Congress in 1841 that considered and passed Senator Benton's "Log Cabin Bill." In effect, the law confirmed title to the land (i.e., prior right of purchase) for up to 160 acres for the "squatter" at the price of $1.25 an acre. As one historian has written, the government was compelled to adopt the measure in order "to make established law and order conform with the lawless and uncontrollable spirit of the American frontier." The pre-emptor had fifteen months to pay, clear some land and erect a dwelling, with at least one window. An actual "Proof" of such work was required prior to the issuance of a patent to the land.

The National Homestead Act of 1862 went even further, providing for free land, if the claimant had lived on the land for five years. It also required some nominal land cultivation and the construction of a dwelling. This legislation reinforced the image of the small American farmer as the cultural and economic backbone of the country. As noted journalist and avid free land reformer, Horace Greeley (of "Go West, young man" fame), wrote in the *New York Tribune,* the Homestead Act embodied "one of the most beneficent and vital reforms ever attempted in any age or clime - a reform calculated to diminish sensibly the number of paupers and idlers and increase the proportion of working, independent, self-subsisting farmers in the land evermore."

Later, in the 1870s, the Timber Culture Act of 1873 and the Desert Land Act of 1877 influenced settler options in the Salt River Valley. The former act provided for an additional 160 acres in exchange for tree plantings while the Desert Land Act recognized that 160 acres was insufficient for Greeley's "self-subsisting" farm in the arid West; the Act allowed up to 640 acres, an entire section of land (a township was comprised of 36 such sections).

Throughout the 1870s, the Phoenix area continued to expand its agricultural base through an expanded canal system and homesteading. There were 93 homesteaders (see Phoenix Homesteaders Master List in Appendix) who successfully obtained patents in the four townships surrounding the fledgling town of Phoenix. In total, these homesteaders secured 103 patents, for several were to obtain more than one patent. The vast majority secured their land through the Pre-Emption Act (57), with the Homestead Act accounting for 25 patents. Perhaps it was simply easier paying the $1.25 an acre and securing the land more quickly. The Desert Land Act was utilized in 15 patents, while only 4 patents were issued under the Timber Act. One patent was a Scrip Warrant and one was a Military Bounty Land Warrant. In total, these 103 patents accounted for 18,450 acres that were homesteaded in the immediate Phoenix area.

Phoenix Townships

The successful patents during this time period were largely around the Phoenix Townsite in Township 1 North/Range 3 East and to its west, Township 1 North/Range 2 East. The Cartwrights' homesteads (at today's 51st Avenue and Thomas Road) were the furthest western patents. Settlement to the north had begun, but only sparingly, due to the lack of canal extensions. The Osborn homesteads (today's Osborn Road) were the northernmost patents. (Only a few of the streets on the Phoenix Townships map were in existence at that time, but simply serve as a guide for where the townships are geographically located.)

The process of homesteading and "proving up" had its challenges in all areas of the West. It must have been an arduous task in the dry Sonoran Desert of the Salt River Valley. Amidst the success of these homesteaders are countless examples of those who were compelled to "relinquish" or abandon their homestead claim, unable to "prove up." A brief examination of the homestead filing history provides a revealing glimpse behind the demanding process.

Relinquishments or cancellations far outweighed successful patents, 152 as compared to 103. A cursory study of Arizona patent history suggest this was likely the norm; less than half of all homestead applicants were successful in securing a patent. In this study of Phoenix in the 1870s, the largest success/relinquishment imbalance occurred in Township 1 North/Range 2 East, where 102 cancellations were recorded in that decade. It is probable that farming was simply not possible where canal extensions had not yet occurred. The first homestead claimants on December 17, 1870, were the Elliott family. James, Robert and William all filed for 160 acres in this township - none secured their patent. Later, James (who was appointed the first Public Administrator for Maricopa County in February, 1871) was a miner in Santa Cruz County in 1884. William died in Casa Grande in 1911, listing his occupation as miner. It is likely that the Elliotts followed the Swilling Party to the Salt River Valley and attempted, unsuccessfully, to turn from mining to farming.

Of the 152 relinquishments, several homesteaders were compelled to cancel certain claims but became successful elsewhere in other areas - Direly Rumburg, James Murphy, John Burger, Sarah Edgar and John Buck. A number of prominent Phoenix settlers were compelled to relinquish claims: John Chenoweth (of the Favorite/Chenowith 1871 gunfight); John Roach and Cromwell Carpenter, saloon keepers; Benjamin

Block of Block and Barnett, merchants (his partner, Aaron Barnett, however, was successful); John Moore, former Yavapai County Sheriff, and Reuben Thomas, Maricopa County Sheriff; George Mowry, friend and business associate of William Hancock; J. M. Sears, who later successfully homesteaded and ranched along the Verde River and maintained a prominent home in Phoenix; Lewis Bailey (of the George Young lynching in 1875); James Murray, whose several daughters married prominent Phoenix settlers and helped to populate Phoenix with their progeny; and Henry Garfias, Phoenix constable and first City Marshal. Of the 152 relinquishments in the 1870s, 11 of those were by Mexican claimants, like Garfias.

In contrast, 7 Mexicans successfully claimed eight patents. Overall, there were 5 female applicants; only two of whom, Sarah Edgar and Emeline Stickney, received a homestead patent. Emeline (age 51) would marry Nathaniel Sharp (age 58), an early pioneer farmer of the Tempe area, in 1878. She continued to live in the Valley until her death in 1904. Sarah Edgar, a single woman, kept her homestead property until 1888, when she sold 199 acres and a share in the Wilson Ditch and donated one acre to School District No. 7. It is interesting to note that she signed these property records with her mark - an "x." This level of female participation was quite low compared to other regional studies of Western homesteading in the late 19th century, where estimated female participation was 10-12%.

One further anomaly is worth touching on. Jack Swilling made a preemption claim in Township 1 North/Range 3 East on December 26, 1870, where he would build his large family home and tend his farming business. Yet, inexplicably, Swilling never received his patent. This did not prevent him from selling his "claim" to William Hellings in 1873 for $3,000. There is no record of Hellings assuming the Swilling claim or paying the Prescott Land Office for the 160 acres.

Continuing with that homestead story, Hellings then lost that land to his partner and early settler, Charles Veil, in 1876. Charles Veil became one of the first homesteaders to take advantage of the Desert

Land Act in 1877, on land adjacent to the former Swilling property. Veil also claimed 160 acres further east that he would later sell to Maricopa County for the State Asylum on the old Tempe Road (Van Buren Street). In his memoirs, Veil also related a homesteading practice often used in the West, particularly by railroad and timber companies. Veil persuaded a "young Swede" who worked for him to file on yet another 160 acres. According to Veil's story, that young man made his Proof and paid the $1.25 an acre. Veil then purchased it from him for $400. Could that have been the homestead of Hans (Albert Theodore) Hanson from Denmark? Charles Veil, a hero of the Civil War and later merchant and land speculator in Phoenix, eventually left Phoenix in 1891.

In Phoenix, as elsewhere in the West, "family" homesteading generally led to some level of financial prosperity as well as to long-term residency in the Phoenix settlement. The willingness and ability of several family members to work together provided a base for the creation of a smaller, cohesive community. Early family settlers included the Starar brothers, the Buck brothers, James and Luke Monihon, and several larger families, including the Issacs, Osborns, Grays and Cartwrights. The latter three families are illustrative of how this family support system proved invaluable. Moreover, the history of these particular settler families provides insight into the journeys pioneers took to Arizona.

The Osborn Family

John Preston Osborn was one of those pioneers drawn to the opportunities of the West. Born in 1815 in Tennessee, he married Perlina Swetnam in Kentucky in 1841, where John was a shopkeeper. They moved to southwest Iowa about 1852; and then after a stay in Colorado Springs, on to Prescott in 1864. The Osborns are known to have operated the first hotel on Granite Street, a two-story frame structure. John also ran cattle on Willow Creek, north of Prescott; and later near Camp Verde and by 1869 on the lower Agua Fria River. Neri Osborn, his son, would later remark, "We gathered the corn by day and the Indians gathered it by night." Ill-health drove them back to the hills and mountains of Prescott in that same year. On January 29, 1870, the *Arizona Miner* reported that "J.P. Osborn and family started Monday last for Phoenix, Salt River." They were following son William's move to Phoenix in 1869 with John Alsap (who had married John's daughter, Louisa but who had passed away in 1867 at the young age of 20).

On December 21, 1870, William Osborn filed a Declaratory Statement, or pre-emption, on 160 acres, adjacent to his brother-in-law, Thomas Barnum (married to sister Jeannette) who filed on the same day. According to his own pre-emption file, John P. Osborn moved on to his land, adjacent to his son on March of 1871, building his house that year (on today's McDowell Road, at 7th Street). In the 1870 Census, John lived with his wife and four children, including William (age 28), on the farm. John Alsap was a neighbor. With the depression of the mid-1870s, they lost this land in 1874, selling to Mary Woolsey (King Woolsey's wife) for $1,000. Next year, they sold another 160 acres to Michael Wormser for $800. William also sold his land in 1875.

John and Perlina Osborn

But the Osborns were not done with homesteading. Son, Neri Osborn, filed for a pre-emption in 1878, at the age of 28, on 160 acres in the Township to the north. Both John and William filed for Timber Act claims nearby (along today's Osborn Road) that same year. In total, by 1887, the Osborn family had accumulated 800 acres through these homestead patents and land purchases.

The Osborns made indelible contributions to the settlement of Phoenix and to the history of Arizona. John was active in the founding of the Phoenix Townsite, serving for a time as the Chair of the Town Association. He was a member of the first Board of Trustees for the School District, established in 1871. John was also active with other Salt River Valley farmers in the late 1870s exploring ways to mutually achieve better grain prices from local merchants. Neri and his wife, Marilla (another Murray daughter), later became the parents of Arizona's future 7th Governor, Sidney P. Osborn, who served from 1940-1948. William, in turn, married yet another Murray sister, Ethelinda, eloping in 1873 against her parents' wishes. Ethelinda was nearly 17; William was 31. They had 11 children from 1873 to 1896. John P. Osborn passed away in 1900; William, who remained a farmer the rest of his life, died in 1927; and Neri who became a bookkeeper, then real estate agent, then accountant, died in 1944. The Osborn/ Murray family descendents continue to reside in the Phoenix area; few other early pioneer families can claim such a distinction.

The Columbus Gray Story

Like other western migration stories to Arizona, this one started in the deep South, but ends with an unusual twist. Born in Florida in 1833, moving to Alabama and then to Arkansas, Columbus Gray grew up in the traditional southern, slave-owning, plantation culture.

Columbus Gray

In 1860, his father owned sixteen slaves, while his brother, Josiah, owned eight. However, the West beckoned him early - with a brother, Columbus headed west for the gold fields of California, then on to British Columbia. He returned to Arkansas in 1859 and later enlisted in the Confederate Army, serving through several horrific battles (including the Battle of Prairie Grove, where he lost his brother, James), enduring imprisonment for nine months, and eventually escaping.

Following the war, Columbus returned to Arkansas and soon thereafter married Mary Norris. In part to assist the health of his sometimes frail wife and perhaps to escape the sorrow of the changing South and seek a fortune once again, in February of 1868, Columbus, Mary and their servant, Mary Green and her child, along with fourteen others (including Josiah Gray, wife and child; Benjamin Patterson, wife and two children; and Hosea Greenhaw, a relative of the Norris family) left Arkansas in a wagon train bound for California. They arrived in Maricopa Wells in August of that year.

As Mary recalled years later, "Lum" went over to the area where Jack Swilling had started the first ditch and farm. "The valley when we first saw it was lovely. There was grass a foot high, and it was fine." In another recollection, Mary declared, "I don't believe I ever saw a prettier place in all my life." They obviously knew something about farming and saw an opportunity provided by the canals off the Salt River. And likely felt the dry climate might be healthful for Mary.

Their journey westward had ended. By 1880, the entire extended Gray family was living at the Columbus Gray ranch (on today's south 7th Street, near Buckeye Road) - Columbus and Mary, Mary's parents, and brothers William and Josiah; as well as Mary Green, servant and cook, who now had four children. The first Gray home was a brush shanty followed by an adobe home and corral. On December 26, 1870, both he and Hosea Greenhaw filed their Declaratory Statements on 160 acres, each. Another early pioneer, John Montgomery (who would marry a Greenhaw in 1876) homesteaded between them.

In Gray's Proof, John Alsap and Francis Shaw were his witnesses. In their statement, the two apologized for the tardiness of the affidavit, noting that "there is no viable mode of traveling [illegible] that the route is infested with hostile Indians." They affirmed that in April of 1870, Columbus had built a "house of adobes with wood" and that "since said settlement, plowed, ditched and cultivated about one hundred and fifty acres." Columbus secured an additional 640 acres through the Desert Land Act in 1882 in the Tempe area. In his filings, he reported that the "whole tract has been irrigated this season but only about 200 acres has been cultivated." The water was provided by a ditch about five feet wide and two feet deep. Columbus Gray affirmed owning four shares in the Tempe Irrigating Canal Company. The land was planted in wheat. Son William stated he had helped "to make the ditches."

William Gray would settle on homestead land at a later date. Josiah Gray homesteaded in the late 1880s along the Agua Fria (in present-day Avondale). Following Josiah's death in 1892, widow Annie Gray secured a homestead patent on her own in 1895 (north of Indian School Road in west Phoenix). The Gray family certainly capitalized on the growth of the valley and the land programs of the federal government.

Columbus Gray's first task was to obtain water west from the Swilling Ditch. It is likely that he and his neighbors - Greenhaw, Montgomery, Ammerman and the Starar Brothers - got permission from Swilling to lay out the "Dutch Ditch" in 1869. Later, in 1874, Columbus was instrumental in the creation of the new Phoenix Ditch Company, an outgrowth of the January, 1874 flood that seriously damaged the Swilling Ditch. While this venture did not prove fruitful, a year later, Gray participated in creating the new corporations to manage the old Swilling Ditch - the Salt River Valley Canal Company and the Maricopa Canal Company. He was also active in politics. He was likely engaged in all the meetings surrounding the new Phoenix Townsite, as he was a signer to the original Salt River Valley Town Association. He would soon own land and property in the Townsite.

In an August, 1876 letter to his family in Boston, George Loring wrote of his visit to the "splendid ranch" of Lum Gray. "he had a fine place comfortable mud house with trees set around it giving the place plenty of shade. he had a negress to do the house work. his wife was the most lady like looking woman I have seen in the Territory ... He [Lum] is a good fellow."

Columbus Gray was appointed in February of 1871 to the new Maricopa County Board of Supervisors; he was not elected later that May. However, one of the first elected Supervisors, M. L. Stiles, resigned two weeks after the election, and Columbus Gray was appointed, serving until November of 1872. That same year, Columbus was the defendant in two assault cases. In 1878, he served one term in the 9th Territorial Legislature. Brother William served as Maricopa County Sheriff in 1899-1900.

The Grays with Mary Green

Columbus Gray passed away at his ranch in 1905 while Mary lived to the age of 90 on the same farm until 1936. They had no children of their own. Their servant, Mary Green had a total of five children in Phoenix - in 1870, 1872, 1874, 1881, and 1886. During those early years, there were no other African-Americans in Phoenix. All of the children were in the Gray household in 1880 and a surviving picture that appears to be from the early 1890s, shows Mary and one of her children at the Gray home. By 1900, they were no longer at the Gray ranch. Mary Green died in 1912. Her son, Jack, changed his name to Jack Gray in the early 1900s (one source suggested that Jack was the only Green child that Mary Gray formally adopted). Jack began work as a farmer, later serving a short time with the Phoenix Police Department in the

1930s. In 1942, Jack Gray, son of a former slave, would sell the last remaining acreage of the Columbus Gray homestead on 7th Street. The Columbus Gray/Mary Green relationship remains a mystery.

The Cartwright Family

This is another intriguing pioneer story of that westward movement following the Civil War. But unlike the Grays, the Cartwrights made it all the way to California. Their journey to Arizona is illustrative of the unexamined exodus of Californians who caught the "Arizona fever" in the 1870s. Their journey to Arizona is one of the few reminiscences preserved by early pioneer Phoenix families.

The Cartwright story began in North Carolina, with the migration first to Tennessee and then to Indiana and finally to Illinois, where Jasper Reddick Cartwright was born in 1837, one of nine children. In fact, his father, Reddick, married three times and had 21 children between 1816 and 1862. It was actually in Indiana that the Cartwright family began their public land purchase history, long before the Homesteading Act of 1862. In Indiana, Reddick procured 80 acres. Following their move to Coles County, Illinois, he received four different land certificates between 1831 and 1838, totaling 240 acres. Not too far to the east, in Sagamon County, Illinois, their famous Methodist preacher cousin, Peter Cartwright, made eight different filings from 1826-1834.

Jasper attended school and grew up in the 1830s and 1840s on the family farm. On March 27, 1857, Jasper married Sarah Elizabeth Riggins. With the advent of the Civil War, Jasper joined Company K of the 123rd Illinois Regiment. They saw significant action, including the devastating battle of Chickamauga and the Atlanta campaign. Over three years, Jasper's regiment lost 219 men, 85 of whom were killed in action. Sadly, brother Levin Cartwright died of typhoid fever, shortly after being mustered out, and just two miles from their Coles County home.

Similar to other returning soldiers, Jasper did not adjust to life back on the family farm. The West beckoned, certainly enhanced by the stories of his brother, Elias, who had been to California and back on several occasions. Another brother, John, a blacksmith, shared this pioneering urge to start anew out West. By the Spring of 1869, John had overhauled their father's old covered wagon and had built a new one.

On April 13, 1869, Jasper and Sarah and their three children; and John and Martha and their four children embarked on the four-month, covered wagon trek to California. The seven children ranged in age from 18 months to 14 years. And both Sarah and Martha were pregnant. Over 2,000 miles later, the Cartwright wagon train rolled into Chico, California. Earlier, in Wyoming, in June, Martha Cartwright gave birth to a new daughter along the California/Oregon Trail. Two weeks after arriving in California, Sarah also delivered a baby daughter, Anna. While Cartwright reminiscences of this arduous journey are scant, what an undertaking it was. The journey included the hot Western prairie, swollen rivers, treacherous mountain terrain, traveling through desert land, and always with the threat of Indian attack. All of this with two of their members pregnant. It was a Western journey that spoke volumes of the pioneering spirit of the Cartwright family. This was not a search for gold; the Cartwright trek was to establish a new life, with greater economic opportunity.

Jasper and his family stayed at brother Elias' wheat ranch for about two years. In 1871, they pursued their own dream of a cattle ranch in Modoc County, Goose Lake Valley, between the Applegate-Lassen cut-off trail to Oregon and the California gold fields to the south. It was a 200-mile trip over rough trail, before they settled at Davis Creek. The nearby Modoc War of 1872-73 created a fear of Indian attacks. But it was the winters of 1873 and 1874, with their devastating snowfalls, that prompted the Cartwright family to move once again.

Perhaps it was promotional literature of land opportunities in Arizona that beckoned. Annie Cartwright Pike recalled, "my parents were afflicted with what they called 'Arizona fever'." In the Spring of 1874, the family set off for Prescott, Arizona Territory. Family memories of this trip were more detailed and vivid. Jasper's family and several others (not Elias or John, whose families continued to live in California for generations) set out under the leadership of George P. Walker, husband of Rhoda Jane Cartwright, Jasper's sister. Jasper's sons, Mantford and Reeves drove the cattle, along with young Thomas Brockman, an orphan Jasper had offered to feed if he would accompany the wagon train (Thomas would later marry Addy Cartwright, Jasper's daughter).

So, back across the Applegate-Lassen cut-off of the California Trail to Winnemucca, once again enduring the 70-mile Black Rock Desert. It was so dry they lost half their cattle, sold the rest and bought more supplies. The Cartwrights probably followed the Humboldt River past Black Mountain to Palisade Canyon before heading south, "thru all the deserts we could hear of," lamented Reeves later. While it is not clear exactly how they crossed down through Nevada, the Cartwright recollections reported reaching Coyote Holes [not too helpful to the historian, for there were "coyote holes" everywhere in the West]. They had been advised to test the waters for poison by the "redskins" (if true, it was most likely the Moapa Paiutes). A short time later a man was murdered at the same campsite. The utmost vigilance was required. A day later, the Cartwright wagon train arrived at the Upper Muddy River, staying there for a week.

From there it was another 60 miles across the Dry Lake Valley desert to Las Vegas. The trail offered little water and no springs. The caravan traveled primarily by night. While Las Vegas in 1870 was but a camp site, with a population of eight, the surrounding valley contained artesian wells that supported extensive green areas and meadows (or "vegas" in Spanish). The Cartwright party rested there for a week. Reeves recalled that trip through Nevada as being more difficult than their original wagon train journey west to California.

Continuing on their journey, within a few days, they arrived at Summit Springs (present-day Searchlight, Nevada). That small water hole there was not what they expected. Some of the party drove the horses to the Colorado River, 15 miles over the hills to the east to rest, graze and drink. They returned to the wagon train with fresh water. Ahead of them lay another stretch across the eastern Mohave Desert to Fort Mojave and a crossing of the Colorado River. It would prove to be a trying time.

Tom Brockman had his horse stolen by Indians at night while he slept with the reins near his arm. In addition, water, stored in barrels lashed to the running gears of the wagon, was still running low. As Mantford recalled in 1934, "That night we lost our way and our teams tired out. My father told my uncle the only thing to do was wait for daylight. This we did. At break of day, Father climbed a sand dune where he spied the Stage road." This was the old stage road from San Bernadino, California to Fort Mojave. "We left our wagon on the desert, put two of our horses on uncle's [George Walker] wagon, put two of the older boys on the two other horses and sent them ahead with canteen to bring back water." The Cartwrights arrived on the western banks of the Colorado River and camped for the night. An old scow, operated by Mojave Indians, ferried them across the river to the Fort.

Seven miles north of Fort Mojave, William Harrison Hardy had settled the town of Hardyville around 1864. By 1866, he owned the Territory-granted franchise for the Prescott and Mojave Road, which became known as the Hardyville Toll Road. It traveled a distance of 165 miles to Prescott. Road toll rates were in the range of four cents a mile for each wagon drawn by two horses, mules or oxen. The Cartwright wagons were drawn by horses. There were extra charges for additional livestock and horse riders. Hardy also freighted goods for the government.

The Cartwright family moved on along the Toll Road, crossing the Black Mountains at Union Pass, then the Cerbat Mountain Range and south to Beale's Springs (near present-day Kingman, this had been the site of an army camp that had protected emigrants and early settlers of the area during the Hualapai War of 1866-1870). When the Cartwrights came through, the Springs was most likely a way station and camp site, having been recently vacated as a temporary Indian agency to the Hualapai Reservation. The Toll Road continued on to Willow Grove (another former military camp) and Fort Rock (formerly J. J. Buckman's stage station, renamed following a successful rebuff of a Hualapai Indian attack in 1866, while occupying his son's play fort on the station grounds). At this point, the road crossed through the historic Baca Float No. 5 along the route of the Amiel Weeks Whipple survey party of 1854, heading southwest through Aztec Pass to Fort Hualapai at Walnut Creek, and on through Williamson Valley and American Ranch to Prescott. The trip passed without incident.

Jasper and Sarah Cartwright

The Cartwrights arrived in Prescott in September of 1874, with $20 in their possession. When they arrived, the Cartwrights would have found a bustling town of perhaps 1500 people (larger than Phoenix), not counting all the surrounding ranches and the multitudes of miners in the surrounding mountains. The new Plaza had been built. The first of many saloons, the Quartz Rock Saloon, along the later-named Whiskey Row, had opened. There was a blacksmith shop, assayer office, the Juniper Restaurant, Prescott's first drugstore (The Pioneer), the Post Office, C. P. Head and Company hardware store, and the sole Goldwater mercantile store in central Arizona. Jasper went to work at the sawmill (most likely the Pioneer Sawmill, the first in Arizona). Reeves ran cattle at the L. A. Stephens Ranch at Point of Rocks. Initially, the Cartwrights camped at Granite Creek, then boarded at one of the Stephens' buildings, finally building a log cabin a mile west of town near the landmark, Thumb Butte. During this short time in Prescott, Jasper homesteaded 84 acres, receiving the patent in 1877.

Something compelled them to move further south, for in December of 1876, Jasper and Sarah and their six children packed up for the last time and headed to the Salt River Valley and Phoenix. In contrast to their previous journeys, this was only a seven-day trip. They camped at Iron Springs, then Date Creek, and Martinez Creek and on to Wickenburg. From here they rode to Seymour and on to Calderwood's Station or Well on the Agua Fria, the last water stop before Phoenix. The Cartwright family arrived in Phoenix on January 5, 1877. They lived in a former adobe granary building, owned by homesteaders, John Montgomery and Hosea Greenhaw. That first Spring they farmed south of town near the Salt River.

Having had success in Prescott, Jasper filed a homestead application for 160 acres in 1877, nine miles west of town, three miles west of the furthest farm, on desert land. This became known as the Cartwright District (near current-day Thomas Road and 51st to 58th Avenues). Jasper received two homestead patents in 1883 and 1888, totaling 320 acres. Son Reeves homesteaded another 160 acres on adjacent land, receiving his patent in 1885. And Thomas Brockman homesteaded yet another 160 acres (Thomas and Addie later moved to California in 1904, as did Reeves Cartwright.)

One of Jasper's patents was through the Soldiers' and Sailors' Homestead Act of 1872, conferred to honorably discharged Civil War veterans, whereby he received his land for only the cost of filing fees. His other patent was through the Desert Land Act under which he paid $1.25 an acre. In that latter application, Jasper provided a glimpse of the property in 1877. He recorded that he moved there in September of 1877, initially living in a shed, built out of forked cottonwood branches, covered with dirt and plastered with mud. In the Spring of 1878, they moved into their adobe home, consisting of two rooms, 14 by 14 feet each. All of this for the Cartwright family of 10. In two surviving letters from Sarah Cartwright, written in late 1877/early 1878 to her mother and father, she reported that "We have got a home here ... a good home." The second letter went on - "We have bilt me a new home with four rooms. We have got a front room, bedroom and a dining room and a kitchen." At the time of Jasper's Final Proof, the family had an orchard of 150 fruit trees and eight acres of alfalfa. Sarah Cartwright wrote about this same time period that "I am a raise chickens now. I have got the finest chickens you ever saw. They say they are worth fifty dollars per dozen ... I have got 10 hens and 2 roosters." In the early 1880s, Jasper was also growing wheat and barley.

In Reeves' Final Proof of his homestead, filed in 1884, he stated - "I have an adobe house, two room, a corral, some outhouses, twenty acres fenced and alfalfa on it. Seventy-five acres in wheat and barley and other crops, also have an orchard and some grape vines." At that time, Reeves had a wife and three children. Neighboring farmer and brother-in-law Thomas Brockman, affirmed that Reeves had built his adobe home in 1879.

Life on the homesteads was all about farming and family. Sarah wrote in January of 1878 that "Jasper has sayed tell you he is heal over head in work. He can not get time to rite timely. Is very ehased [exhausted] now. We do not make as much as we did almost a year. Jasper does not idle one minute ... we have got a big family to take care of. We are a coming as Jasper says we can justifies ourselves." In a revealing reflection, despite the tasks of the farm and family, Sarah wrote, "Sometimes I feal so Lonely ... but I always look to mi Savior in my troubles and I find relief. I feal like some time I will not be here long to see the troubles of this world. All I as is to be prepared to go at my Master's call. I wish we was able to send after you and Mother." Loneliness out on the furthest western edge of the Phoenix area was probably not openly expressed but is certainly consistent with other Western women homesteader writings and recollections.

The nearest potable water was on the Issac homestead, over three miles away. The family hauled barrels of water from there for several years. In addition, the Cartwrights had a "dobie hole" similar to other settlers. It was a 20-30 foot diameter hole, 3-4 feet deep and lined with adobe bricks. Rainwater was channeled from ditches into these holes and used as water tanks for stock as well as for family. Charles

Cartwright also recalled hunting for antelope and quail nearby. "When the country was dry and there was a lot of sage brush, people set traps for quail ... wild geese and ducks were plentiful ... ."

The Cartwright family initially attended Central School in Phoenix until 1879, when the one-room adobe schoolhouse in Issac opened. The children walked and rode their horses to that school. In 1884, the first Cartwright School was built on land donated by Thomas and Addy Brockman. Future Judge, Alfred Lockwood, was their first school teacher. In 1901, Sarah Cartwright's brother, John Riggins, arrived from Illinois to teach at the school. He later was elected Maricopa County School Superintendent and then held the State position of Superintendent from 1923-1945. The Cartwright School District still exists today.

Water, of course, was the key to their long-term farming interests. The Cartwrights helped organize the Grand Canal Company and owned four shares (or 400 inches of water allocation). The men hand dug the canal to Grand Avenue by 1878. The Cartwrights and other farmers extended it west to their land by 1880. Sarah wrote that "He [Jasper] has bot a water rite in a dtich. He has to give five hundred dollars for it. It is going to put us behind ... ."

However, the Cartwright family continued to prosper. Mantford Cartwright, starting with a cattle stake from his father, began his cattle business in the early 1880s as a teenager, moving his stock up to the grassy hills of the Cave Creek area, with a small cabin, then a ranch and homesteaded land at Seven Springs. He began a Cartwright ranching tradition that would last nearly 100 years. The Cartwright family contributions in Phoenix to education, church and the wider community were well-known throughout the twentieth century. While Sarah died in 1906 and Jasper Cartwright in 1912, their legacy lives on through several generations and family lines in the Phoenix area. In fact, one descendent still lives on the original Cartwright homestead.

Early Mexican Homesteaders

Canal location was also critical to pioneering Mexican farmers. In fact, many Mexicans worked on these early Salt River Valley canals alongside Anglo settlers. The role and participation of Mexican homesteaders is often overlooked. While it was noted earlier that there had been 11 cancellations/relinquishments by Mexicans in the 1870s, there were also 8 successful Mexican homestead patents in the immediate Phoenix area. Of these eight, five were in Township 1 North/ Range 2 East; the other three were east of there, south of the Salt River, close to the early canals (a number of Mexicans had settled even further east of there in the 1870s, in what would later become Tempe and several Mexican families successfully homesteaded land in that area, primarily in the 1890s). Four patents were secured through Pre-Emption, three through the Homestead Act and one through the Desert Land Act.

Pedro Sotelo and Nicholas Sanches likely both worked on the early Mexican Ditch, later named the San Francisco Canal (three other Mexicans who worked in that same general area during the 1870s relinquished their claims). Nicholas Sanches (variously spelled with an "s" or a "z" in his Homestead file), reported in his Proof that he had settled on the site in 1871. This is consistent with his filing of a Declaratory Statement in Prescott in that same year. Pedro Sotelo and Jose Peralta both affirmed in 1878 that they had known Nicholas for seven years. They also stated he had cultivated about 140 acres of his quarter-section, and his property consisted of an adobe house, 35 feet by 16 feet, a well, 50 shade trees and "a supply of water for irrigating said land." Records indicate that by 1881, Michael Wormser owned the property.

Pedro Sotelo came from a very prominent Mexican family. Pedro's grandfather served as the Commander of the Presidio of San Ignacio de Tubac from 1813-1814. In 1820, he was assigned to oversee the nearby Tumacacori Mission. His sons, Tiburcio (with his wife, Manuela) and Pedro, came to the Valley in 1870. Tiburcio and Manuela settled over near the fledgling community of Tempe (which, by the 1890s, became the Sotelo Addition), while Pedro settled to the west in the Phoenix area along the Salt. Both apparently even assisted pioneer Tempe settler, Winchester Miller, with his canal work. Winchester, a widower, became so enchanted with Manuela's daughter, Maria, that he courted her for several years, marrying her in Tucson in 1873 (Maria was 14, while Winchester was 38) at a Catholic church, most likely at Manuela's insistence.

Meanwhile, Pedro was likely farming in the early 1870s, but it was not until May of 1877, shortly after the passage of the Desert Land Act, that he filed Application No. 16. One week later, he assigned those 400 acres to Michael Wormser for $200. Thus, when the final Proof was submitted in April of 1880, it was actually executed by Wormser, as assignee. Wormser stated that no crops had been grown on the land prior to 1877, to which William Hancock attested.

However, Pedro was most enterprising. In October of 1877, he filed a Pre-Emption claim for 160 acres north of the Salt River, west of the Phoenix Townsite, adjacent to the former homestead of Guadalupe Ortega (who had sold the land to Barnett and Block in in 1873 for $300). Pedro received this patent in 1878, upon payment of $200, perhaps with the cash paid to him by Wormser the previous year. He sold this tract to Wormser, as well, in August of 1878 for $500. Perhaps Sotelo was more interested in the buying and selling of land.

Finally, in 1889, Pedro sold yet another 110 acres of land he owned south of the Salt River, again to Michael Wormser, but this time for $2,000. It is not clear where Pedro lived during these times or whether he even actually farmed. However, it is clear that this Mexican settler, who apparently did not write in English, certainly learned enough to participate in the real estate market of early Phoenix.

Jesus Otero was the most prominent Mexican landowner in Phoenix in the 1870s. From his homestead filing to land and buildings in the Phoenix Townsite, Otero worked successfully with the predominant Anglo community as well as his own Mexican community. Jesus was likely in the family tree of the early Spanish family of Don Toribio de Otero, who received a land grant from King Charles of Spain just north of the village of Tubac in the late 1700s. His grandson, Sabino Otero, expanded these early holdings after the Civil War into the largest cattle empire in southern Arizona. Jesus, born in the State of Sonora, Mexico, in 1833, married in 1859; migrated north at some point; and settled in the Phoenix area in October of 1872.

At that point, he filed a Declaratory Statement, claiming 160 acres west of the Phoenix Townsite. Real estate records indicate he had actually purchased that tract from William Hellings, suggesting that Hellings perhaps had, himself, acquired a previous claim. In fact, Otero paid $900 cash, a sizeable sum in those days. He recorded the deed in 1878 to support his claim to the land. In 1879, Otero informed the Florence Land Office he desired to change his claim to the 1862 Homestead Act. He clearly did not wish to pay for the land twice.

In his Homestead Proof, Otero reported that he had a wife and seven children. He reported that he had gone to California in 1848, moving to Arizona in 1863. The Otero family lived on the homestead in a two-room adobe. He reported that the house was built in 1870 (perhaps this was the former home of David Cooley, who had filed an earlier claim on the land). Otero had cultivated about 130 acres, growing wheat and barley. Edward Buker and Augustin Ronquillo were his witnesses. Both had known Otero for 10 years, placing his actual arrival in the Salt River Valley at closer to 1870. Augustin had sometimes even worked on Otero's homestead over the previous seven years. Otero received his patent in 1880.

In the 1880 Census, the Oteros lived next to Miguel Peralta and his family, on Washington Street. Mabel Hancock recalled the Otero home as a one-story adobe, two rooms deep on Washington Street and four rooms along 1st Avenue. She referred to them as a "prosperous Mexican family." Jesus Otero would send his three sons to college in Santa Clara, California. The eldest daughter, Rafaela, was a school teacher. Their in-town residence was likely a boarding house, as well. The 1881/1882 Town Assessment records show Otero owned 10 lots, eight of them in Block 79, on the northwest corner of Washington

Street and 1st Avenue. Later in the 1880s, he sold five of those lots in Block 79, raising $15,000. At the time of his death in 1901, Jesus Otero left to his family several lots, $3,060 in cash and over 1,000 head of cattle, grazing on the range near Ft. McDowell and the Verde River. In 1943, his son, Arthur, then living in Los Angeles, sold the Otero family's remaining two lots in the Phoenix Townsite.

Michael Wormser

The tale of homesteading in Phoenix would not be complete without a profile of Arizona pioneer, Michael Wormser. More than any other Salt River Valley homesteader, Wormser became a voracious land speculator. It is somehow fitting that his story appears after those of the Mexican homesteader and farmer, for their lives and destiny were so intertwined. Michael Wormser, fluent in four languages, learned how to manipulate the homesteading process, water rights, farm lending practices and the courts to become, at his death, the largest landowner in the Valley.

His story began in France in 1827, where he was born into a Jewish family. At age 30, he made the fateful decision to head to California in search of gold, following in the footsteps of his cousin, Benjamin Block. In fact, his cousin even paid for Wormser's steerage from New York to San Francisco. By 1859, he had joined Block at San Luis Obispo, working in the livery business. When this venture proved ill-fated, Wormser then took to peddling, buying and selling horses, lending out his profits, and investing in agricultural land.

With opportunities appearing to be too limiting, Block now invited Wormser to La Paz, Arizona, in 1863, where they jointly operated a general store (with initial assistance from Issac Goldberg). When the mining boom fizzled, Wormser was captivated by the lure of gold in north central Arizona. He not only staked a number of mining claims, but also began to peddle goods to other miners. By 1864, Wormser had started the first general store in Prescott. It was here that he started his practice of providing credit to local area ranchers for merchandise and supplies, collateralized with real estate mortgages. The *Arizona Miner* carried a story in 1873 that Wormser and his partner, Aaron Wertheimer, had opened a new store in Phoenix. And who had previously settled in Phoenix? - cousin Benjamin Block, and his partner, Aaron Barnett. Wormser's initial efforts seemed promising; he sold goods to farmers, was paid with grain and would resell the grain for a profit. When grain prices tumbled in 1875-76, Wormser closed his store and began again. He turned to farming, irrigation and real estate.

Homesteading provided him with the avenue to new opportunity. Wormser applied for a number of patents on his own. He quickly responded to the new Desert Land Act of 1877 with his own claim on 240 acres on the south side of the Salt River in April of 1877. He had become a naturalized citizen in Prescott in 1871 (a requirement for a homestead applicant), under the name Miguel Wormser.

Wormser reported in his Proof that he had sown about 150 acres in 1879, growing wheat and barley (he planted the same crops on the former Sotelo tract in 1879, yielding 200,000 pounds of grain). By this time, according to his Proof, the San Francisco Canal was largely under his control. It ran eight miles from the Salt River to the point where it entered his land. In his file, Wormser appended two notable exhibits: one, his assignments of land from Pedro Sotelo of 400 acres and that of Hans Yaeger of 500 acres, adjacent to Sotelo; and two, a recent court decision rendered in his favor against Jesus Gonzalez (a neighboring homesteader) and other Mexican farmers, granting an injunction against them to refrain from using his canal water. Wormser provided evidence, apparently satisfactory to the Court, that he controlled the rights of the Canal with ownership of 12 of the 14 shares, with the other two owned by Mariano Balesteros. Wormser's two witnesses were William Hancock (who handled a good deal of Wormser's legal matters; and whose son, Henry Hancock, was a foreman for Wormser at times) and Herbert Patrick. Wormser received his patent in 1882.

He received a second patent in 1891 for another 160 acres along the San Francisco Canal. Of note, Pedro Sotelo and Pancho Mesa were witnesses, both farming nearby land. In his Proof, Wormser reported to have a house, 45 feet by 16 feet and to reside there "for whole period [1880-1885] except when absent in business, never six months at a time." Wormser stated he brought the house, built in 1872, to the land.

Finally, Wormser received his last patent in 1894, this one a Timber patent, south of the San Francisco Canal. His witnesses were William Hancock, Pedro Sotelo as well as Francisco Meza and Manuel Ortiz, both nearby homesteaders who received their patents in 1892. Wormser attested that he planted 1529 cottonwood trees to the acre, planting 10 acres. He had a tenant in charge of the timber cultivation. Wormser paid his $200 and received his patent in 1894.

Michael Wormser

As is clearly evident, Wormser acquired most of his land through dealings with Mexican farmers, dating back to the 1870s and continuing for twenty-some years. Here is how it worked. Wormser provided seed and supplies to Mexican farmers along the San Francisco Canal as well as the water necessary to harvest a crop, and in return secured a mortgage on their property. In the summer farmers grew corn, beans, watermelons, pumpkins, greens, sweet potatoes and onions for their families and for sale in Phoenix. Then, the cash crops of wheat and barley were planted. As Wormser related in a court case involving water rights: "I give them all the water for the poor peoples ... I furnish the water, lands, animals and tools ... That is the advantage they got, and that is the reason they stick to old Wormser." By all accounts, Wormser drove a hard bargain in a desert farming business susceptible to grain price fluctuations, Salt River flooding and drought. Some have contended that Wormser's practices were simply unscrupulous.

Of the eight Mexican homestead patents of the 1870s, four were acquired/conveyed to Wormser during that same time period; three of those along the canal. The Sotelo and Sanchez transactions have been detailed, although it is not clear if Nicholas Sanchez received any compensation. Gabriel Fimbres sold his 160-acre homestead to Wormser for $1300; Manuel Ortiz did likewise in 1892 for $1500, retaining 25 acres. In the latter case, Wormser had taken a mortgage against the Ortiz property in March of 1892 in the amount of $1280 and purchased it outright in July of that same year. Another of Wormser's previous homesteading witnesses, Francisco Meza, also sold his land to Wormser for $1500. In that same year, Wormser acquired another 90 acres from Anita Salazar for $1200; she had finished her husband's patent process on 160 acres following his death. In 1893 Wormser acquired 100 acres from Clara de Soto, a widower, and Henry Garfias, for $275. With all of this land under his control, it was likely that many of these same farmers may have rented Wormser's newly-acquired farming property.

Michael Wormser acquired land from Anglos, as well, and at bargain values. Even his own cousin, Benjamin Block and partner, Aaron Barnett, only received $275 for 640 acres in 1875. That same year, Wormser paid John Osborn $800 for 160 acres. In 1878, he purchased 160 acres from Thomas Taylor for $500. Later that decade, he secured the assignment of the Yaeger homestead, with no record of actual compensation, albeit there is a record of a $400 lien that Wormser had on the Yaeger property.

In the 1881 Maricopa County tax rolls, Michael Wormser had one of the highest property valuations, encompassing over 3000 acres, two-thirds of which were south of the Salt River. His wealth and his fiscal conservatism led him to his election to the Board of Supervisors for a four-year term (1880-1884), even serving as Chair for a time. That is the sole public role that Wormser assumed. His name achieved some notoriety as the named plaintiff, among several, in a significant canal and water rights lawsuit that resulted in the landmark Kibbey decree of 1892.

By the 1890s, Michael Wormser had become something of a curiosity. By this time he was focused exclusively south of the Salt River along the San Francisco Canal. He ran his agricultural empire alone from a dilapidated warehouse on Jefferson Street, that was widely considered to be an eyesore. He appeared to live the life of a pauper. Upon his death in 1898, Michael Wormser had liquid assets of only $100 in gold coin. His dwelling contained a bedstead and mattress, one sofa, one upholstered chair, three wooden chairs, one wardrobe, one dresser, one table, one bookcase and one stove. And he owned nearly 7000 acres of land, most of which was sold out of his estate to Dwight Heard of the new real estate venture of Heard and Bartlett for $132,000. His cousin, Benjamin Block, received nothing from Wormser's will or estate. As one historian noted, "Rather fittingly, he died in the middle of a lawsuit."

Wormser Office

Homesteading in the 1870s

Looking back, homesteading laws drove land ownership and farming in Phoenix and the rest of the Salt River Valley. By and large, the claimants were not land speculators but committed farmers. Those who discovered that farming in the desert did not lead to immediate profit and wealth, such as Darrell Duppa, either relinquished their claims or sold soon after receiving their patents.

The more surprising result was the extent of long-term land ownership by the majority of the 1870s' homesteaders. Where data was available on the 93 homesteaders, nearly 40% sold their land within five years for a variety of reasons, including death. The majority, however, continued to farm into the 1880s and beyond - the Osborns, Issacs, and Cartwrights among them. The early homesteaders' future was also impacted by increasing population growth, compelling residential growth to move out in all directions from the original Phoenix Townsite. This phenomenon created opportunities for the first subdivisions of Phoenix. Not surprisingly, several of the earliest subdivisions were from the early 160-acre tracts - Neahr's Addition (George Buck's former homestead); the Dennis Addition; the Murphy Addition; the Montgomery Addition; and the Capitol Addition (Simon Novinger's homestead that was sold to Collins and Sherman, early developers of street railways and real estate), all in the early 1880s. Several pioneer homesteaders even became some of Phoenix's first developers.

Homesteading continued to spur the outward growth of Phoenix for the balance of the 19th century. From 1880-1889, 90 patents (43 of those were homesteaders who claimed land in the 1870s) were issued in four townships surounding the Phoenix Townsite, with the numbers increasing to 259 for the period 1890-1899. Homesteading played a vital, yet often ignored, influence on this settlement pattern.

CHAPTER FOUR
The Phoenix Townsite

May 1, 1871. This may well be the most important date in Phoenix history. For on this day, voters would decide the location of the seat of the newly-established Maricopa County. It was a bitterly contested campaign. Rumors were circulating that Mexican votes were being bought. Jim Favorite, a candidate for Sheriff, had been killed in March by his political opponent, J. A. "Gus" Chenowith. Friendships and business relationships were divided over the issue. Fortunes were at stake, depending upon the site selected. Would voters favor Mill City, the original settlement site (generally located near present-day 30th Street, between Roosevelt and Van Buren Streets, comprising the Swilling Ranch and the Hellings Mill); or the George Mowery Ranch (further west near present-day 16th Street) and the site of the popular McKinnie saloon and store; or a 320-acre site just a mile further west, promoted by the new Salt River Valley Town Association, adopting the early settlment's name of "Phoenix" in October of 1870?

The seeds of that rivalry had begun perhaps as soon as the canals began to extend west from the original Swilling Canal and farmers claimed land beyond the original farms of 1868. The early settlers knew that the establishment of a townsite was important to advancing commerce and growth. And, it was anticipated that the next meeting of the Territorial Legislature in early 1871 might consider the creation of a new County and set in motion the selection of a County seat.

In August, 1870, there were newspaper reports that "two towns were being laid off within the week." In October several meetings were held, by Republicans and Democrats, as the political fever of the impending

November elections drew closer. The former group "voted" to select the site near McKinnie's saloon, a 160-acre site claimed by James McKinnie. John Olvany also ran the post office out of that building. It was the social center of the young community. McKinnie and Cromwell Carpenter operated a popular eating house and saloon. William A. Hancock was asked to begin the surveying process, necessary to establish a townsite, including obtaining title from the federal government and "disposing of lots to actual settlers," according to the *Arizona Miner.*

Later that same month, on October 20, the Democrats held a community meeting at the home of John Moore to purportedly bring some order to this conflict. Chaired by John T. Alsap, they appointed yet another selection committee, comprised of John Moore, Darrell Duppa and Martin P. Griffin. A week later, the committee recommended the 320 acres in the northern half of Section 8 (present-day boundaries being Van Buren on the north; Harrison Street on the south: 7th Street to 7th Avenue; hereinafter referred to as the "Phoenix Townsite"). They also endorsed the name of Phoenix.

The story of the actual purchase of the Phoenix Townsite is largely dependent upon the story of Neri Osborn, as recorded by historian Thomas Edwin Farish. He related that Johnnie Moore wanted to donate a 40-acre site but that "father [John P. Osborn] always contended that forty acres was not enough, and told them that three hundred and twenty acres should be set aside for the townsite. In the fall of 1870 ... father and I visited the present site of Phoenix to get a load of wood. We found two men quarreling over the quarter section which lies directly east of Center Street. Father asked the men why one did not take the quarter in dispute and the other the quarter adjoining to the west. This proposition was refused by both, and it occurred to father that the two quarter sections would make an excellent townsite, and, after a little coaxing, the parties to the dispute agreed to quit claim their right, title and interest to the quarter section upon the payment of twenty-five dollars to each ... At the meeting, the following day, the fifty dollars was raised by popular subscription, and what is now the thickly settled portion of Phoenix, worth millions, was surrendered for a pittance."

It is generally assumed that John Olvany and John Moore were the parties involved in the dispute. Actual pre-emption claims were not permitted for formal filing until December of 1870. At that time, Jacob Starar filed his claim on the southeast quarter of Section 8, while Darrell Duppa (under the name Brian P. D. Dupper) filed on the southwest quarter in February of 1871. Hence, there is no tangible record that either Olvany or Moore had actually begun the process of pre-emption by building on land in Section 8. In the 1870 Census (filed in August of that year), it was recorded that Olvany was actually living on McKinnie's property, probably, as was customary in those days, in the back of the post office. John Moore, a former Sheriff of Yavapai County, had recently relocated to Phoenix and was not in the Census. However, Neri Osborn's account does refer to Moore owning a place west of the McKinnie saloon (which is apparently confirmed by a deed referring to an "old timey" house which preceded the Townsite but was built on what would become Washington Street, next to Hancock's "first" Townsite building). Both gentlemen, however, were involved in this political process and knew what was at stake. John Moore was even on the aforementioned selection committee. Not only did they release whatever pre-emption claim they may have had for that "pittance;" but also, neither individual secured a homestead claim elsewhere (John Moore had claimed a quarter section closer to the Salt River in 1871 but later relinquished it; Olvany appeared to have staked his future to the saloon business).

With the Townsite formally selected, this Democratic group created the Salt River Valley Town Association to carry out the tasks associated with the patenting process. John Alsap, James Murphy and Joseph Perry were selected commissioners. Within two days, William Hancock (who had performed some partial surveying for the McKinnie proposal), assisted by Osborn, James Monihon, and Thomas Barnum, began surveying the 320 acres. Hancock was to be paid by "subscription," monies to be raised by the Association to be later credited against his own lot purchase. The work and leadership of Alsap and Hancock were critical to the legal establishment of the Townsite and the procurement of the federal patent to the land, a process with which the town of Prescott was also concurrently engaged. It is not surprising that Hancock would often be called the "father of Phoenix" while Alsap would not only be one of the first Commissioners but would also serve as the first City of Phoenix Mayor after its formal incorporation in 1881. Either could qualify for that "father of Phoenix" title.

It has been suggested that these Democrats had supported the Phoenix option because it was generally level, above the Salt River floodplain and devoid of Hohokam ruins. Recent archaeological evidence documents that a sizeable Hohokam village existed at what became known as Pueblo Patricio, and would have certainly contained evidence of ruins. The Townsite also had a thick grove of mesquite trees covering a portion of its western half. It is likely that neither quarter section was being actively farmed.

The Phoenix Townsite was advanced not because of its Democratic leadership (Democrats already outpolled Republicans four to one in the Salt River Valley) nor due to its lack of archaeological ruins. The Phoenix site was proposed because of its immediate proximity to the pre-emption claims of this new leadership. Such important supporters as Osborn, Duppa, John Montgomery, the Starar brothers, James Murphy, and Columbus Gray and their support for the Phoenix Townsite is inextricably linked to the location of their farms. The Osborns (John and his sons, William and Neri) had claims immediately northwest of Section 8. Duppa and Jacob Starar were immediately south. James Murphy and Andrew Starar had farms to the southeast. And Lum Gray's ranch and the Montgomery farm were directly below those of Duppa and Starar.

The composition of the Salt River Valley Town Association and its first members was also evidence of the changes occurring in the political landscape: Darrell Duppa, William B. Helling and Co., [Aaron] Barnett and [Benjamin] Block, Thomas Barnum, James Murphy, John T. Dennis, William A. Holmes, James W. Buck, Jacob Starar, John T. Alsap, Columbus H. Gray, Martin P. Griffin, James M. Elliott, Joseph C. Perry, William Rowe, Michael McConnell, David Twomey, Charles

C. McDermott, Edward Irvine, John P. Osborn, Andrew Starar, Paul Becker and James D. Monihon. Nearly all of the "claims" of the above members were west of Mill City and west of McKinnie's saloon and land. And then there was the case of Hellings and Company, obviously abandoning its political allegiance to Jack Swilling and Mill City. Barnett and Block were recent merchant newcomers from Wickenburg and certainly coveted land in the proposed Townsite. Murphy and Dennis had recently opened a business just east of the proposed town and would be one of the first businesses to move into the Townsite. The absence of any Mexican farmers in the membership of the Association is glaring.

In spite of financial and legal risks (the Association did not exist under law and had no legal right as of yet to the 320-acre site), the Association wanted to move forward with land sales, to cement in the popular mind the validity of the Phoenix Townsite. On December 2, 1870, the Land Office at Prescott began to accept formal pre-emption/ homestead applications in the Salt River Valley. It was vitally important for the Association to assert its rights to the Townsite by proceeding with land sales. With only the eastern half of the Townsite surveyed, the Association announced "GREAT SALE OF TOWN LOTS" in the *Weekly Arizona Miner* on December 17, 1870. The first sales of lots were held on December 23 and 24, selling 63 lots for $20-$142.50. The first lot was sold to Judge William J. Berry, the Register of the Prescott Land Office. Hancock completed the survey in the Spring of 1871, assisted by Omar Case, a civil engineer.

This momentum carried over to the political arena. John Alsap, a member of the Legislature from Yavapai County, steered a bill through both the House and Council to establish a new Maricopa County from the southern portion of Yavapai County and make Phoenix the County seat. Governor A. K. Safford's proclamation creating Maricopa County occurred on February 14, 1871. He also named Phoenix the County seat but with the actual location to be subject to voter approval in May.

The balloting on May 1, 1871 resulted in the Phoenix Townsite being chosen as the County seat with 212 votes, followed by Mill City with 150 and Mowry's Ranch with 62. Not surprisingly, Salt River Valley Town Association members figured prominently in the first Maricopa County elections: John Alsap was elected Probate Judge (a good position from which to pursue the federal patent); Thomas Barnum - Sheriff; William Hancock - Surveyor; and James Elliott, Coroner. None of the three County Commissioners, however, had been Association members - M. L. Stiles, James Young and Francis A. Shaw. Shaw had a preemption claim just west of the Townsite. Stiles, for some unexplained reason, resigned shortly after his election; Columbus Gray was appointed. The popular George Mowry, a friend and business associate of Hancock, was elected Treasurer.

As for the fortunes of the other potential County seats, their importance was short-lived. Major James McKinnie never did receive a patent on his claim. His partner, Cromwell Carpenter, became the new saloon keeper in the Old Brewery on Washington Street a year later. Social and saloon activity shifted to the new Townsite. McKinnie's fate is not to be found in public records. Similarly, Mowry never gained title to his ranch; it is likely that farming was not where his interests lay. However, in addition to being Treasurer, he remained the assistant in Hancock's post office that also moved to the new Townsite in a building built by Hancock. Mowry served as sheriff for several years in the mid-1870s and as Postmaster in 1879 and again in 1881. Mill City survived in town history for perhaps another decade at which point the mill closed down.

Townsite Governance

The Townsite Commissioners were naturally focused on the patent process and the continued sale of town lots. Under the federal Townsite Act of 1867, following the completion of the survey, an actual plat and declaratory statement had to be filed with the General Land Office in Prescott, then processed forward to Washington, D. C. for the federal patent. However, the Arizona Territory had never passed operational procedures to implement townsite law.

In February of 1871, "An Act Relating to Town Sites" was passed by the Territorial Legislature. Inexplicably, Judge Alsap did not file the Declaratory Statement until one year later. Then, with the passing of yet another year, in March of 1873, Alsap filed for the federal patent on behalf of the Salt River Valley Town Association. It can only be surmised that the concurrent legal townsite process of the town of Prescott was somehow slowing down the Phoenix Townsite process. In November, 1873, Judge Alsap, acting as Trustee, purchased the 320-acre Townsite for $400, or $1.25 an acre; the formal federal patent was issued on April 10, 1874. Then, it was not until May 18, 1875, following a year of legal review, adjudication and certification by the Townsite Commissioners, that Judge Alsap finally issued valid deeds to those who had purchased land, beginning in December of 1870!

In the midst of this uncertainty, a new set of Commissioners (Martin Griffin, John Alsap and William Hancock) moved forward on land sales. In order to generate cash in January of 1871, the Commission actually switched to fixed prices -- $5 for inside lots; and $10 for corner lots; obviously, a major reduction in what had been paid just three weeks earlier. Furthermore, in 1871, the Association agreed to provide other lots for the public good, in addition to the County Courthouse block and the City Plaza block -- two lots were to be deeded for a public school, one for a Masonic Hall, two for the Methodist Episcopal Church South and an entire block to William Bichard for the new flour mill. Bichard did indeed erect such a facility; it burned down within a year; was not rebuilt and yet curiously did not revert to the Town.

Regrettably, there are limited archival material relating to the workings of the Association. Land sales continued to be a high priority. In late 1875, the Association was still selling lots, but now required that $100 worth of improvements be made within 12 months prior to the granting of title. Obviously, and not surprisingly, land had been and was still being purchased for land speculation. Also, in that same year, the Commissioners held the first ever sale of 120 lots with delinquent assessments. Some deed records from the late 1870s suggest that vacant land sales by the Association were still valued in the $5-$10 range. In an 1879 report to the *Phoenix Herald*, A. D. Lemon reported that other lots had been donated for various purposes -- four lots to the Methodist Episcopal Church; one lot to the Catholic Church; and that Blocks 55-58 had been set aside for the community graveyard. Lemon reported that only 8 blocks of the 92 and several scattered lots had not been sold. Public records show that several entire blocks were then sold to individuals in 1879 and 1880 for $80.

In October of 1875, a general meeting of the town was called to discuss the fiscal affairs of the Association. A number of key Townsite leaders were present: John Alsap, Edwin Irvine, William Hancock, James Monihon, J. A. Parker, M. Wormser, James Murphy, A. Goldman, J. J. Gardiner, John George, J. A. Burger, and Daniel Dietrich. John Smith, Burger and James Cotton were elected to serve as Trustees. A visible change in leadership had occurred - Alsap and Hancock were still ever present but now larger property owners (Monihon, Gardiner, George, Cotton and Wormser) are joined by new merchants (Goldman, Burger and Dietrich). Interestingly, Monihon proposed, seconded by Alsap, that incorporation of the Town be pursued; it was defeated, 8-4. The group even adopted some new regulations, providing some insight into their primary concerns at the time:

1. "Administer" the town's property "in the best interests of the Town."
2. "Use the moneys belonging to the Town in an economical manner."
3. "Procure" the necessary water rights and "cause the same to be equitably distributed."
4. Construct and maintain the ditch system "in a clean and serviceable condition."
5. Dispose of remaining town lots

In 1875, much of the Phoenix Townsite was still covered with brush, mesquite trees and desert vegetation. As George Loring wrote to his family in Massachusetts upon his arrival in Phoenix in 1876, "the houses are all dobie, which make a cheap comfortable house. the Town is laid off in squars with good wide streets, a dich from the main dich running up each side with cotten wood trees close togeather on the side of the dich. it gives the street a very good appearance." At the time, only a few blocks were clearly defined roadways, suitable for stage-coaches, buggies and horse travelers. Washington Street was probably well-defined from 1st Avenue to 3rd Street. A few connecting streets, as well as Jefferson, Adams and Monroe, were likely cleared.

At a meeting of December 13, the Commissioners (now consisting of John Smith, Daniel Dietrich and William Hancock) invited proposals to clear Washington Street of brush and timber and dig a ditch on its south side from Courthouse Plaza to the western end of the Townsite (present-day Seventh Avenue), and to create a drainage ditch to the south. Stagnant water was always a problem and this was done to alleviate that problem as well as to encourage development on the west end of Washington Street. Three proposals were received from William Hancock, Thomas Childs and Inocente Garcia. The bid proposals appeared to be very close. Hancock was awarded the bid - $$44.70 for the Washington Street ditch; $18 to clear Washington Street; and $130 to construct the southerly ditch on the western edge of town. Apparently, a sitting Commissioner could bid on a Town project and not be considered a conflict of interest. John Cotton was in charge of the maintenance of the ditches and drainage on Washington Street; John Burger had responsibility for Adams and Monroe Streets. In November of 1875, Cotton was paid $129.62 and Burger $146.32 for their services, likely employing Mexicans at $1.50 a day.

Ditch maintenance had always been important to Town sanitary health. The Commissioners entered into annual agreements with the Salt River Valley Canal Company to procure water from a point at the eastern edge of the Townsite. In 1875, Hancock was requested to post a warning notice that "any person hitching horses to shade trees or where they will obstruct or injure the ditches will be prosecuted to the full extent of the law." As George Loring noted in another letter to his family in Boston, conditions were still not acceptable: "the dich water, dogs bathe drink and do other healthful duties in it. it is used for a universal wash basin. the Mexican Women wash clothes in it. horses drink out of it. Dirty vessels of all kinds ... are washed in the afore said ditch ... A horse was laying dead in the dich. a good deal of the water stands in place stagnant." And in January of 1878, the *Salt River Herald* reported that 40 inches of water had been secured for the town ditch, reminding readers that there was punishment for those "casting or washing filth into the village water ways."

In March of 1878, the same paper ran an editorial deploring the condition: "Many of the adobe holes [outdoor privy or outhouse], alley-ways and even places in the streets are simply pest heaps where rotten filth and garbage send up effluvia engendering disease." The editor even appealed to the County Board of Supervisors to clean up the area, possibly even by the use of jail inmates, prior to the onset of warm weather. On March 23, the Association Board ordered that "no person hereafter shall take from any street, alley, lot or block belonging to said Town any dirt, sand or gravel for any purpose [there must have been an adobe building boom going on] ... all persons to keep sidewalks and ditches in good condition ... no persons shall turn the surplus water passing their property into any adobe hole or bathe or throw any filth into the ditches." The problem did not go away. Another public notice issued by the Association in July again referred to "cesspools of filth ... stagnant pools of water ... unclean privy" and required clean up or be subject to prosecution as a "NUISANCE."

In June of 1879, an article in the *Phoenix Herald* reiterated the need to clean out the canals and ditches. "We have the handsomest village in Arizona ... let not its bright prospects for the future be blasted by a want of proper care in those things that go to make it a healthful, cheerful place." Later in September, another report noted that ditch water had to be turned off and advised all property owners to remove the "filth and garbage" from the ditch. The Town Association Report of 1879 (issued by Lemon) did not allude to this on-going issue but noted that there were 9 miles of street ditches and "36 plank flumes" had been installed at street crossings in the last eight months. Lemon also reported that water rights had again been secured to irrigate trees and shrubs in the business and residential areas of town.

Early Phoenix Leadership

Throughout the decade of the 1870s, there were farmers, merchants, landowners and canal builders who influenced the course of Phoenix history. With respect to formal community leadership, two pioneers stand out - John Alsap and William Hancock. The short biographies included here provide a glimpse into the life journey of these two pioneers and the leadership character evidenced in their roles and contributions.

John T. Alsap

John Alsap was another of those early Arizona pioneers who came to Arizona from California after mining fortunes eluded them. One significant difference - Alsap's keen mind stood out. He had educational training far beyond his contemporaries, including a family traditon of learning (his father was a minister) as well as his own medical training in the early 1850s in Marion, Ohio. These learned traits were readily recognized by his fellow pioneers.

After arriving in Prescott in 1864, Alsap served as company surgeon in the famous King Woolsey Apache campaign. As the newly-founded Arizona Territory was organized, Alsap was appointed its first Treasurer. To make ends meet, he continued to mine in the area and even partnered with John Roundtree in opening the town's first saloon. He was also involved in the creation of the Prescott townsite. Alsap served two terms in the Legislature, representing Yavapai County. Clearly, he had made a quick impression on the early Prescott community.

In 1869, Alsap and John Osborn's son, William, ventured to Phoenix. Here, John chose to enter into the law (admitted to the bar in 1872) and combine legal skills with his already apparent leadership skills. In the early Territorial years, any white male who was at least 21 years of age and "of good moral character" could be admitted to the practice of law in the Territorial courts. Alsap immediately delved into canal business, becoming counsel for most of the ditch companies, including Jack Swilling's canal ventures. He led the Legislature initiative to create a separate Maricopa County; was appointed the first Probate Judge for Maricopa County and later District Attorney; and was elected to two more terms in the Legislature in 1875 and 1879, serving as the Speaker of the House in the latter session. He was an initial incorporating member of the Salt River Valley Town Association. His last County office was as a member of the County Board of Supervisors from 1879-1880.

John T. Alsap

John Alsap's most enduring contribution to the future progress of Phoenix involved the establishment of the Phoenix Townsite and the development of the first public school. As previously described, his leadership and legal capabilities were indispensable in obtaining the patent for the Phoenix Townsite. Throughout the balance of the decade, he oversaw Town land sales as well as the conveyance of proper legal title to lot owners. John was likely equally proud of his role in establishing the first public school district in the new town and serving as its first Superintendent. In the mid-1870s, he married Anne Murray, yet another eligible daughter of the Murray clan.

The vaunted reputation of John Alsap certainly led to his election as the first Mayor of the newly-incorporated City of Phoenix in 1881 (beating another old pioneer, James Monihon, by seven votes). John was also a successful farmer, being one of the early pre-emption claimants in 1870, and a Townsite landowner. In the 1881/82 Assessment, John Alsap owned 10 lots (including his law library in the valuation) and several tracts of land in three different townships. He sold his homesteaded property in 1881 (where he had his original adobe home on McDowell Road) for $1500. He was still dealing with several mining claims as late as 1882. John Alsap was 56 when he passed away in 1886, having laid "the foundation for our happy homes which now dot our valleys," stated one of the press obituaries. Always committed to public service, even just prior to his death he had been nominated for County Treasurer. John Alsap led this pioneer settlement of a few former miners and farmers into a mature town in just over a decade.

William A. Hancock

William Hancock - soldier, town planner, lawyer and homesteader. He established the townsite plan that would forever impact the development of Phoenix. Like thousands of his generation, William, along with his brothers, John and Henry, left their hometown of Barre, Massachusetts to seek their fortune in California in 1853. While the two brothers would return to Massachusetts, William remained in California, most likely as a rancher or even engaged in mining, north of Sacramento. He mustered in with the California Infantry in 1864 along with his friend and future business associate, George Mowry. And in the process, they entered the Arizona Territory.

Hancock's company went to Fort Yuma and then to Fort McDowell in July of 1865. At war's end, he was honorably discharged and then joined the Arizona Volunteer Infantry. A year later, he had left the Army and was employed as Assistant Superintendent, then Superintendent of the post farm at Fort McDowell, earning $150 a month and serving until 1868. Early 1870 found William, now 39, as post trader at Camp Reno. By the summer of 1870, he had moved once again - this time to the Salt River Valley.

William and George Mowry opened a store in the vicinity of the Swilling ranch. Their ad in the *Arizona Miner* read, "We have opened a store near J. W. Swilling and intend to keep on hand all kinds of groceries, provisions, dry good, clothing, and a general assortment of merchandise." This business venture was short-lived, for soon thereafter, he was appointed Postmaster and moved to Murphy's store on the old Tempe Road (on today's Van Buren Road, just east of 7th Street).

At this point, the fall of 1870, William quickly emerged as a key figure in the competition over a new townsite and the location of the County seat, ultimately providing surveying services to the Phoenix Townsite and becoming an incorporating signatory to the new Town Association. He went on to purchase one of the first lots in the Townsite and subsequently, in early 1871 built the first adobe commercial building, measuring 15 by 30 feet, in the Townsite on the north side of Washington Street (near the west side of today's 1st Street). It initially housed the Post Office (where Mowry was in charge of day-to- day operations) and the first merchant in the Townsite, William Smith, who made a quick profit and departed for California after only eighteen months. In the latter part of 1871, Pete Holcomb established the first butcher shop in Hancock's store. In the rear of the lot, Hancock stored his "fees," as he was often paid in wheat and barley for his services. In October of 1871, William and James Monihon built a more substantial adobe, south of Washington Street (on today's 1st Avenue). It was largely rented to the County for their offices and for the jail. William Hancock had wisely chosen the winner in the Townsite competition.

While he continued to do surveying work, Hancock now entered the practice of law, being admitted in 1872. He and John Alsap likely had the bulk of the legal work in those early years. Hancock served as County District Attorney from 1871-1875, then as Probate Judge from 1875-1879. Similar to Alsap, he was both a Secretary and shareholder in several canal companies. Hancock was active in the Town Association from its inception, serving as Commissioner for a number of years during the 1870s. He also served in 1880 as the County Superintendent of Schools. With such a stellar commitment to public service, Hancock would soon try his hand at farming.

William and Lillie Hancock

William now had a family to consider as part of his future. In 1873, at the age of 42, William married Lillie Kellogg, the 18-year old daughter of a prominent ranching family, in a ceremony at the Kellogg ranch. Lillie must have had some education prior to the Kelloggs arriving in Arizona, for surviving letters show proper spelling, good punctuation and a quite readable cursive style. In 1874, Lillie gave birth to a son, Harry. The Hancocks were living at 33 Cortez Street (now 1st Avenue), one block south of Washington, just west of the Courthouse Plaza.

Their 5-room adobe had 18-inch thick walls, with a roof of cottonwood logs, covered with brush and eight inches of earth. The kitchen and dining room were later located in a detached adobe. The lot eventually had trees, grass, roses and a corral. Lillie's mother was a mid-wife to Lillie's second child, Mabel, born in 1876. In those early years, they even employed a Chinese cook, who was living with them in 1880.

Mabel described her father as a "man of enterprise." This was an accurate portrayal, with his several business ventures, law practice and farming. In 1876, he unsuccessfully pursued a land patent for 160 acres next to the farm of Lillie's brother, Owen Kellogg. Not to be deterred, he likely continued to farm the land and in 1878 pursued an unusual, but legal, path to procure the land - a Bounty Land Warrant from the Department of Interior for 160 acres. The Military Bounty Land Act of 1855 entitled soldiers to bounty land as a reward for their military service. A Daniel Higdon had served with the Mississippi Militia in the War of 1812. His children had the assignment for Daniel's bounty land warrant. On March 29, 1878, the children sold it to Charles D. Gilmore of Washington, D. C. for an undisclosed sum. On July 3 of that same year, Gilmore sold the warrant to William Hancock, again

Military Bounty Land Warrant

for an undisclosed sum. On July 25, Hancock submitted the warrant to the Florence Land Office and it was approved on July 31, 1878. That was clearly the quickest process of securing a homestead patent by any applicant in the 1870s. It is likely that Hancock was already threshing his wheat at the time, for early Mormon stories from the Mesa settlement to the east, tell of working for Hancock during the summer and newspapers referred to his new threshing machine.

With the passage of the Desert Land Act of 1877, Hancock pursued additional farm land by filing on 640 acres in April of 1877 in far west Maricopa County (current-day Avondale). King Woolsey, and merchant, Charles Stearns, vouched for his character in the application. With his Final Proof submitted in 1880, Hancock documented his ownership of water shares in the Grand Canal Company. His patent was awarded in June of 1882.

At perhaps the height of his farming ventures in 1883, the *Arizona Gazette* provided an overview of Hancock's holdings. 600 acres at the far west side farm were planted largely in wheat, with 100 acres in barley and 20 acres in alfalfa. A 160-acre farm was rented to W. H. Smith. Hancock leased 640 acres and had a half interest in the Veil crop. Then, it all changed so quickly.

With a serious downturn in the grain market and likely over-extended, Hancock suffered some several financial losses. In 1884, with even his colleague John Alsap suing him on behalf of a client, Hancock turned his assets over to his law partner, Charles Tweed, including his farm land and most of his town lots. He lost nearly everything.

But like other pioneer stories of fortunes won and lost, William Hancock started once again. In 1887, at the age of 58, he made claim to 160 acres south of the Salt River, along Michael Wormser's San Francisco Canal. On this occasion, he utilized the Soldiers' and Sailors' Homestead Act of 1872, taking advantage of his 10-month service with Company K of the 7th California Regiment in the Civil War. In his application, Hancock noted he had sold the land secured through the Bounty Warrant. He had moved onto this land in June of 1887, without his family. He affirmed that he had made a "constant presence and residence without any other home ... I have boarded and slept sometimes in the house of my wife [Lillie] in the City of Phoenix." His testimony revealed that he was often absent for six weeks each winter "while Salt River was too high to ford. I was practicing my profession in Phoenix and I could not afford to buy ferryage - $3.00 per trip." He noted his children had been on the farm "some" and "my wife a short time in April and May of this year [1889]."

William had moved into an existing old house, which he repaired and expanded in the winter of 1887 and spring of 1888. The main adobe house with shingle roof was 38 feet by 15 feet, with a 15 by 17 foot "wing." There was also a 16 by 20 foot cabin for "laborers," a stable and corral. Hancock estimated the value of improvements at $720. He also owned "2 plows, shovels, axe, pitch fork and buggy ... 4 horses and 8 chickens." The house contained "3 beds, 1 stove, 5 chairs, 2 tables, 1 ice box, 1 wash stand. 1/2 dozen plates, 3 cups and saucers ... ." While he had cultivated 100 acres in wheat and barley, they were "not yet threshed." He rented a portion of the land to Francisco Angulo, beginning in September of 1888, who resided there with his family. Hancock made the Final Proof in July of 1889, paid his $200 ($1.25 per acre) and received his patent in June of 1890.

The ensuing decade, Hancock was involved with James Monihon and the Ormes in the Agua Fria Water and Land Company. He had opened up a real estate office with his partner, Charles Tweed. He wrote papers on water issues of that time and wrote numerous letters to Congressman Newlands of Nevada who was sponsoring national reclamation legislation. Hancock, along with others, saw this as vital to the future of water and irrigation in the Salt River Valley. Three months after William Hancock's death in 1902, Theodore Roosevelt signed the National Reclamation Act into law.

In most cases of these prominent male pioneers, the story would end here. Often little is known of the pioneer women who were vital to the settling and civilizing of these western towns. Lillie Hancock's story has been concealed by historians and family members for well over a century. Her daughter, Mabel Hancock Latham, recounted the saga of the Kellogg family journey from California in the early 1870s, noting that Lillie, at age 16, rode all the way on horseback. Two years later, she was married; within months, she was pregnant with their first child.

Mabel, born two years later, described her mother as a "natural born nurse," assisting with the smallpox scare of the mid-1880s in Phoenix; providing aid to a woman who had almost drowned; and caring for someone with pneumonia [a possible reference to Aggie Loring]. She also recalled that Lillie was a "great reader," reading Kate Greenaway's books to her as a child (Kate Greenaway was a prolific English writer and illustrator of children's books. She is most well known for her recreation of the nursery rhymes of Mother Goose, published in 1881). In the early 1880s, Lillie was also active with the Literary Association.

All of this ignores, however, the tragic dynamic within the Hancock family. William Hancock, in his 1889 Proof above, attested that he generally lived separate from his wife and children from late 1887 to 1889. In his attached Affidavit, William provided more information - "My wife has been in feeble health and more or less afflicted mentally by her physical condition for the past 8 years. In March of 1886 she was adjudged insane and for five months was in confinement. Where although she had not recovered her condition was such that I took charge of her myself." Lillie declined to come onto this new homestead claim and in July of 1887 left for California and stayed there for nine months, perhaps with Kellogg relatives or maybe, even William's sister, Catherine, who lived in Sacramento. Hancock continued in his Affidavit that in 1889, "when her condition became such that it was again necessary to place her in the Asylum where she still remains [July, 1889]." Even Francisco Angulo's testimony indicated he knew that Hancock's wife was in the Asylum.

Anecdotal information suggests she may have been admitted to a private sanitarium in Stockton, California even prior to 1886. Both the Territories of Arizona and Nevada had contracts to send their insane to the Pacific Hospital of Langdon and Clark. Maricopa County Supervisors, along with the County Probate Judge, were responsible for approving cases of insanity, upon the recommendation of a physician. Hancock, himself, had overseen several cases of insanity during his term as Probate Judge in the late 1870s.

Official public records reaffirm Hancock's Affidavit, for on January 14, 1886, one year before the new Territorial Asylum was slated to open on east Van Buren Street (on Charles Veil's former homestead), two associates of William Hancock went before Probate Judge Joseph Campbell to petition that Lillie B. Hancock, age 31, be declared insane. One witness, Charles A. Givens, was a law partner with Hancock and had known Lillie for four or five years. He provided the following testimony: "I know her to be an exceedingly amiable and modest woman of more than ordinary intelligence and character. Within the last few weeks, I have met her often and she has shown a very marked condition of insanity. She has come to talk about some business affairs, talking very wildly and insisting upon certain things, and speaking in a low tone and manifesting great excitement ... Whenever she could do, she would get a horse and buggy or go out on foot in the daytime and at unreasonable hours of the night without the company of friends and going whenever she could do so by herself ... During the absence of her husband a little while ago ... such fears were entertained by her friends that she was kept under constant surveillance, and I was compelled to recall her husband while he was engaged in important business abroad. Once during this time, I was reliably informed, she procured a pistol and threatened to use it upon some persons unless they gave up to her a bottle of whiskey in their possession. I was informed that the pistol was taken from her by her brother-in-law by force. I am sure she is at any time liable to do herself or others injury unless restrained. I have seen her the last few weeks, and it is apparent to me she is more and more insane every day."

The other witness, Louis Chalmers, corroborated the recent condition of Lillie - "I have known Lily for about a year. Up to the past two weeks, so far as I know, she was sane. During the past two weeks, she has labored under various business matters that were absolutely improbable, and at other times she wished me to transfer all of her property to get money to assist friends ... She stated that the parties to whom she wished to convey did not want the property, but that she would make them take it. She talks wildly on various subjects ... She would leave me business to attend to, but the next time I would see her would have no recollection of the matter."

Lillie was examined by Doctors Mahoney and Thibodo who concluded: "We testify that she is insane. It is dangerous for her to go out at large by reason of insanity. The said insanity is likely to prove permanent." With that recommendation, the Judge gave his order on March 23, 1886, "I do hereby order that she be delivered into the custody of her husband, William A. Hancock, to be by him placed where she may be properly treated and cured, subject to the order of the Board of Supervisors." It is curious that William provided no testimony in the case. It is not clear if William transported Lillie to the California sanitarium although his Affidavit reported that she was confined for five months. She was admitted into the new Territorial Asylum with her episode in the 1888-1889 time period.

Insanity was taken seriously in the West. It was considered a political plum that the State Asylum was to be located in Phoenix. By 1880, several different official categories of insanity existed: mania, melancholia, monomania, paresis, dementia, dipsomania and epilepsy. But the physical symptoms were many and varied and quite subjective when it came to the female and to the testimony of the male complainants. Today, these unusual behaviors might be characterized as bipolar disorder and prior to that manic depression. At this juncture in history and into the twentieth century, it was just insanity. Several cases in the early 1900s that warranted admittance into the Arizona State Asylum were characterized by depression from pregnancy and/or childbirth, melancholy during menstrual periods, incessant or even incoherent talking, epilepsy, and nervousness leading to lack of sleep. This was indeed very broad latitude.

While Lillie was admitted several times during this period, the 1900 Census revealed that she was living at home with the entire family, Harry and Mabel included. While William passed away in 1902 to deservedly glowing tributes for his contributions to the young pioneer settlement, Lillie's troubles were not over. In both 1904 and again in 1906, her son, Harry, had her readmitted to the Territorial Asylum for the Insane. Harry has been characterized by family members of being estranged from his father; most likely, from his mother, as well.

Daughter Mabel did not recount any of this in her reminiscences, but rather had fond memories of her mother. Perhaps Lillie's mental issues somehow were managed, for there is no further public record of her purported insanity. In 1917, Lillie bought land in the Chester Place Addition, on North 2nd Avenue; was able to borrow $2,000 on the land in order to build a house; paid off the mortgage in 1926; and quit-claimed the property to Mabel in 1933. In that same year of 1917, she loaned the McNeil Company, a local printing company, $5,000 and was repaid three years later. By 1930, if not earlier, Mabel and Lillie were living together on 2nd Avenue. They continued to do so until Lillie's death in 1943 at age 88, succumbing to pneumonia at St. Joseph's Hospital, where she still wore the wedding ring that William had given her back in 1873.

Upon her death, Lillie was hailed as a pioneer in the papers of the day, with no mention of family strife or insanity. Who knows the internal struggles that Lillie endured during those early pioneer years and beyond? It is testimony to Lillie's character and spirit that she persevered through her troubles and her multiple confinements in the Asylum to still raise her children, often with William away and/or living separately from her, and maintain her love for her husband up to his death and beyond. Pioneer life was not for the faint-hearted - the summer heat, the ever-present dust, perhaps loneliness and of course, William's financial struggles through a good portion of the 1880s. It is this complexity, the messiness of life, that is often ignored by family histories. This story of William and Lillie Hancock provides some needed perspective on the difficulties some women and couples faced and endured through those pioneer times.

EARLY TOWNSITE DEVELOPMENT

William Hancock's 1871 survey plat covered an area one mile in length and a half-mile in width. The 320 acres were laid out in a typical grid pattern, and included entire blocks reserved for a County courthouse and a City plaza, quite similar to that recently adopted in nearby Prescott. It is probable that without formal training, Hancock's vision was shaped perhaps in consultation with Alsap, who had similar experience in Prescott.

The Townsite contained 98 blocks, most of which were 300 feet square and were divided into 12 lots (See Phoenix Townsite map in Appendix). Individual lots were generally 50 feet by 137 ½ feet. Blocks (excluding the two reserved sites) were sometimes interlaced with alleys. Hancock and others must have been aware of the negative impacts on town development where access to interior lots were denied. The plat laid out eight main streets, running east-west and fifteen north-south streets. Washington and Jefferson Streets were 100 feet wide; the remainder were 80 feet in width. The former streets were named after Presidents, while the latter were named after Indian tribes, a Spanish explorer

(Cortez), and an Aztec ruler (Montezuma). These latter names would be changed to streets and avenues in 1893. (For the ease of placing actual locations, the 1893 street names are used.)

Phoenix was an adobe town, similar to Tucson. Shipping lumber from Prescott, with high costs and poor roads, simply was not practical. Sun-dried adobe bricks cost $20 per thousand in the early 1870s, while labor was inexpensive. By the middle of the 1870s, it became more common to plaster some of the exterior and interior walls. Floors were hard-packed earth; later improved with wood flooring. The flat roofs were made of saguaro ribs as well as cottonwood and/or mesquite wood, combined with ocotillo sticks and brush, covered by a layer of mud and later, lacquered canvas. Leaking was a common problem.

Washington Street Scene

Monsoon storms wreaked havoc on some of these makeshift roofs. Adobe buildings, often referred to as "houses," were both business and living quarters. The business would naturally open to the sidewalk or street, while the living area was one or two rooms to the rear, with a fireplace for a stove and a privy or "adobe hole" for bathroom purposes. There might be a corral in the rear for their horses. Ditches ran in Washington Street and other side streets.

Early Phoenix would be characterized as a mixed-use community. Saloons were next to the Courthouse. A blacksmith shop might be next to a school. Large livery stables were located in the center of town. Only the cemetery was far removed from the Town center.

Hancock Store

FIRST BUILDING IN PHOENIX, ERECTED IN 1871, ON PRESENT SITE OF THE VALLEY BANK.

In 1872, the Phoenix Townsite business activity was centered along Washington Street. It was shaded in part by cottonwood trees, initially planted by James Monihon. The business district was generally confined to three blocks along Washington Street, from 1st Avenue east to 2nd Street, including Hancock's first building. J. J. Gardiner's building, Phoenix's first hotel, was a block further east. Jesus Otero's lodging house, meat market, and personal family residence was at the northwest corner of Washington and 1st Avenue. Further west was uncleared mesquite and paloverde. The first school was two blocks north of Washington Street on Central Avenue. Bichard's flour mill, Subiate's meat market and Barnett and Block's store, warehouse and freighting operation were on Jefferson Street.

The *Tucson Citizen*, reporting in April of 1872, identified the following types of businesses: 4 stores, 2 saloons, a bakery, a brewery, 2 blacksmiths, and 2 carpenters. Subsequent research documents that there were also two restaurants, three butchers, a law office, a doctor's office/

drugstore, the courtroom (in the Hancock/Monihon building) and a post office. No physical church structure would be built until 1878.

The town had now become a fledgling center of trade and commerce. Murphy and Dennis had relocated to the Townsite. Even after his mill burned down in 1871 over on Jefferson Street, William Bichard still ran a store for a time. Hyman Menassee had moved over from Wickenburg with his general store. Miguel Peralta's store occupied a prime corner at Washington and Center (Central). William Smith still had his store in the Hancock building. Pete Holcomb, the town's first butcher, was also in the Hancock store. "It was in truth an original meat market, for Pete merely killed the steer, cut it in quarters, and hung them up. All customers had to cut off what they wanted, furnishing their own knives, and pay from twenty-five to thirty cents per pound for it. In those days only one beef was consumed in one week."

Julius Buerlein ran the first bakery, while A. H. Peeples, Matt Cavaness and George Roberts (all from Wickenburg) established the first brewery. Their saloon, the "Old Brewery", was operated by Cromwell Carpenter, former partner of Major McKinnie. Frank Cosgrove ran a blacksmith shop in the rear lot of the brewery. The other saloon was operated by Johnny Roach, at Washington and Central. Dr. Thibodo's office and likely his drugstore were both next to the Roach saloon. It is probable there were other drinking establishments at the two "eating houses" as well as at Johnny George's Capitol House located next to the Hancock building. The *San Diego Union* reported in March of 1872 that Phoenix " is a smart town ... contains many houses; also stores, workshops, hotels, butcher shops, bakery, courthouse, jail and

Washington Street Cottonwoods

an excellent school ... Lately hundreds of ornamental trees [cottonwoods] have been set out ... will give the town the appearance of a forest city ... the Salt River Valley will be the garden of the Pacific Slope and Phoenix the most important inland town."

Land Ownership Patterns

The Hispanic influence on the Townsite is often overlooked. But property records show that Hispanic settlers were very active in Townsite land purchases/sales throughout the 1870s. Otero, and for a brief time, Subiate, were early businessmen in the Townsite. Sacramento Granillo, as another example, was an early purchaser of six lots in the Townsite, inexplicably (perhaps losing them to tax delinquency) transferring those lots in 1875 to Michael Wormser. Clemente Romo was another early landowner, but sold his property to Michael Goldwater for $3,000 in 1873 (there must have been an adobe on that site; and yet, that was still a high price). Romo owned several other lots but held none by the 1881/82 Assessment.

Over the decade, these Hispanic land transactions occurred throughout the Townsite. But there were concentrations - in the southeast corner, along Madison and Jackson Streets (Blocks 37 and 38; See Phoenix Townsite map); along Monroe, from Central Avenue to 5th Street in Blocks 3, 6, and 7 (the Catholic Church would build in Block 4 by 1881); and in Blocks 79 and 82 along the western end of Washington Street. By 1881, actual land holding in Blocks 38 and 82 had virtually disappeared. Thirty-five Mexicans owned 44 lots, 10 of them held by Jesus Otero, largely in Block 79. Several Mexicans still owned land in Block 37 as well as Blocks 3 and 6.

Examining property valuation records, Miguel Pesqueira, the tinsmith, was the most prosperous, with a $1900 valuation, with $1,000 of that in "stock" or inventory. Jesus Otero's land and improvements were valued at $1655, while Elijio Ochoa's property (3 vacant lots) amounted to $850. Dennisa Corella owned 1 lot, 4 horses and a wagon, valued at $745. Tranquilina Corella, who was very active in real estate in the early 1870s, owned just one lot in 1881. Other active land traders like Thomas Badillo, Granillo, Romo, Miguel Peralta, and Carlos Talamantes owned no land in 1881. Some had their land taken for delinquent taxes; some must have moved on; and at least two, Miguel Peralta and Thomas Badillo, had passed away. City Marshall Garfias owned no land but had 8 horses, 1 wagon, 2 sets of harnesses and 1 saddle, valued at $806. The Swilling women (widow Trinidad and daughters Matilda, Georgia and Leila) no longer owned the 12 lots in Block 82 that had been transferred to them by Jack in 1874.

The other minority group in the Townsite were the Chinese, arriving in larger numbers in the 1878-1880 period. While there were six Chinese taxpayers, three of those simply had $100 in restaurant fixture valuation. Hei Wing owned the western half of a lot in Block 78, while Sam Wing owned a single lot in Block 8 and had "stock in trade" for a total valuation of $1,000. And then there was William Holland, a Chinese emigrant from New York City - he owned 20 feet of frontage in lots 8 and 9 and all of lots 1-4 in Block 20. He also owned 3 lots in Block 75. His total valuation amounted to $2,000. In the 1880 Census, William listed no occupation (although he owned and operated the Cosmopolitan Restaurant in 1878 and perhaps later) and was living in a dwelling with nine other Chinese. His son, Joseph, lived elsewhere in the Townsite. William's wife, Ellen, with whom he held his property, was not listed.

In contrast to the limited holdings and property wealth of both Mexicans and Chinese, the Anglo merchants and landowners dominated the property tax rolls. Excluding merchants who generally controlled one to five lots, 13 Anglo property owners controlled 262 lots, the equivalent of 21 Townsite blocks. The largest property holders were the estate of J. A. Parker (39 lots), who passed away in 1878; Rebecca Linville (37 lots), the wife of farmer Hiram H. Linville; James Monihon (31 lots); John Cotton (27 lots) and Edward Irvine (26 lots). Other landowners with 10 or more lots included several prominent Phoenix leaders - John Alsap, A. D. Lemon,

Granville Oury and two recent newcomers, Daivd Balsz and Martin Kales, the new banker in town. Land and development speculation began early in the frontier era.

CHAPTER FIVE
The Merchants of Washington Street

Across the West, settlement brought demand for goods and services. Access to the finer goods of San Francisco or from the East was surely a reminder of their connection to a more civilized existence. This was particularly important to pioneer women, with childhood memories of easier times. Mercantile stores offered the opportunity to socialize and as one western merchant commented, "I have often seen a hard-worked country lady come into a store and inquire for all the handsomest good in the stock, and admire them, comment on them, take out great strips or pretty patterns ... fold them ... drape them ... Her face illumined with pleasure at the splendor of such material. Bright, harmonious colors, and fine fabrics, over which she would draw her tired hands caressingly ... ."

For others, it was simply having access to any quality goods. Mary Gray, arriving in the Salt River Valley in 1868, felt this deprivation from the outset. She recounted that the closest goods were in Wickenburg (fifty miles) or in Maricopa Wells (twenty-five miles): "When we wanted merchandise, about all the men in the valley would have to go to Wickenburg for it, and maybe they could get a piece of bacon about a foot long, and six inches wide, for the whole settlement. I was one time without shoes, and Mr. Duppa was going over to Maricopa, and I asked him to bring me a pair. He brought me a pair of sixes, and at that time I wore twos. I told him they didn't fit me exactly, and he said that it was all he could get, and a sight better than going bare-footed."

Mary Gray was delighted when James Murphy opened his store, the first in the Valley, on the "lower road from Wickenburg to Camp McDowell" (near the intersection of today's Van Buren and 9th Streets) on the northwest corner of his homestead. He soon entered into partnership with John T. Dennis, who homesteaded and farmed just north of Murphy. James Murphy had come to the Valley in 1868, having been a trader at several Arizona mining camps, including La Paz, Weaver, Black Canyon, Big Bug and Wickenburg. Dennis had been a miner in La Paz and later along the Hassayampa River. He worked out of Wickenburg from 1865-1868 as a freighter.

Their first advertisement appeared in the *Arizona Weekly Miner* in February of 1871: "will keep constantly on hand and sell cheap for cash, all articles needed by Farmers, Mechanics, Teamsters and Housekeepers." They moved to the Phoenix Townsite in 1872, joining William Smith, who had opened the first store there in July of 1871. The *Tucson Citizen* had reported that "At Wickenburg I met Mr. William Smith and family with teams en route from Los Angeles to settle on the Salt River. He had a stock of goods with him. Stocks of goods are now adays quite a feature everywhere in Arizona."

By 1872-1873, there were several mercantile stores located in the Phoenix Townsite, and nearly all along the broad boulevard of Washington Street, with its cottonwoods and ditches - Murphy and Dennis, Menassee and Company, Barnett and Block, Wormser and Company, Peralta, H. Morgan and Company, the Goldwater brothers and Edward Irvine. Albeit outside of the formal Townsite, William Hellings was a vital merchant in the farm economy, through his flour mill along the Swilling Ditch. Hellings opened his mill in 1872. All of this mercantile activity for a town of perhaps 500-750 population, including the surrounding farmers and their families.

Who were these merchants who contributed so much to the economy, the vitality and even the politics of growth in this fledgling community? While they certainly were a diverse group of individuals, several facets to their merchant journeys stand out. First and foremost, they were risk-takers, moving from one market opportunity to another. Several had lost all of their goods in transit, in the Colorado River or even to Apaches. Several had declared bankruptcy, only to start over. For a number, their journey began in California, then over to the Arizona Territory and the short-lived boom towns along the Colorado River. Every merchant trader, above, with the exception of Irvine, worked out of La Paz for a time in the 1860s. Several were also directly engaged in mining ventures while providing goods to mining communities around Wickenburg or Prescott.

As a result of following boom opportunities, several merchants had other store operations prior to opening their branch in this new Phoenix town. Peralta kept his store in Wickenburg. When Wormser moved to Phoenix, Aaron Wertheimer, his partner, managed the store in Prescott. The Goldwater family's main operation continued to be in Ehrenburg, when they opened their store in Phoenix in 1872, buying out the stock of Hellings when the latter chose to focus more on the mill operation with his brother, Edward. Henry Morgan continued to operate his ferry and trading post on the Gila River, south of Maricopa Wells, into the 1880s.

These merchants obviously saw value in partnerships - Murphy and Dennis; Menassee partnered with Julius Goldwater for a time; Barnett and Block; Wormser and Wertheimer; Peralta and Frank Purcella in the late 1870s; Henry Morgan with Dan Dietrich, until the latter's murder by Indians in 1880. Hellings also partnered with Edward Grover in the early 1870s and later Charles Veil. Managing stores, operating freight teams, and nurturing a customer base required a pooling of capital and a division of labor.

Another characteristic of several of these merchants was their Jewish and foreign-born heritage. Hyman Menassee was from Prussia. Aaron Barnett, Benjamin Block and Michael Wormser were from France. The Goldwaters hailed from Poland. This strong tradition of successful Jewish merchants would continue with the later arrival that same decade of the Goldmans and Goldbergs.

With such competition, it is perhaps not surprising that there would be some market shake-up, particularly with the recession of the mid-1870s. Menassee was the first to go, closing his branch but a few months after opening. Barnett and Block sold out to Wormser in the mid-1870s. They moved into the freighting business out of Tucson. Shortly thereafter, even Wormser was forced to close both the Phoenix and Prescott stores, following Wertheimer's death in 1874. Peralta and Purcella later sold their stock to Adolph Goldman. Peralta then continued with his own store at the corner of Washington Street and Central, until its closing in 1881. Murphy and Dennis dissolved their partnership in the late 1870s, whereupon Murphy moved to Tempe and opened a general merchandise store and corral. Both would later benefit in the mid-1880s by the real estate development on their neighboring homesteads.

Little research has been conducted on the freighting business of the Arizona Territory. Prior to the coming of the railroad, freighting teams traveled all over Arizona. As a result of that use, the Territorial Legislature placed a special emphasis on road building projects. Even later in the decade, after the arrival of the railroad, freighting continued to be important to remote communities in the Arizona Territory, only then the trade route likely began at the railroad depot. Supplies were freighted in "prairie schooners," drawn by twelve or sixteen oxen, horses, or mules. Loads might be as much as 45,000 pounds. They brought an assortment of goods to town and generally hauled out grain on the return trip. Many merchants freighted their own goods such as Murphy and Dennis and Barnett and Block. Others might have used local Phoenix freighters like John Lutgerding (a wheelwright from Germany via Wickenburg), F. M. Fowler, Chenowith and Fenter, or Cosgrove and Cavaness. Matt Cavaness came to Arizona in 1864, settling first in Prescott and by 1872 in Phoenix. Cavaness and Cosgrove were partners in a saloon and ran their freighting operation out of their wagon and blacksmith shop, as did John Lutgerding and his new associate, George Luhrs. While Cosgrove died in 1875, Cavaness continued to freight throughout the Arizona Territory well into the 1880s. He, like others, not only carried merchandise to towns but also grain to military posts and ore from mines.

The freighting business spurred other supporting businesses, including blacksmithing, wagon/carriage repair, and the livery business. John Burger and George Hamlin were well-known; Burger served as one of the first City councilmen in 1881. James Monihon and Albert Henshaw had their own livery and feed stables on Washington Street. The Phoenix Flouring Mill (run by John Y. T. Smith) was competing in the late 1870s with the Salt River Flouring Mill, operated by Charles Veil. These ventures were critical to the farm and to the freighting companies carrying grain.

Freighting could be a dangerous business in these early pioneer days. In 1865, while hauling supplies from Ehrenburg to Prescott, Wormser was struck by an arrow "in the fleshy part of his anatomy nearest the saddle." The *Arizona Miner* commented, "Our time-honored friend, M. Wormser ... returned from a trip ... [however] his old friends ... failed to honor him with the customary salute in the rear." Matt Cavaness related in a later recollection "that many a time he has gone through McDowell Canyon with his hair standing as straight as the quills on a porcupine fearing that each minute would be his last on earth." Hyman Menassee was even killed by a freighter in Wickenburg in 1875, as their argument over prices escalated into a gunfight.

Freighters operated out of all major markets in the Territory - J. M. "Crete" Bryan out of Wickenburg; Charles Hayden out of Tucson, then Tempe; Tully and Ochoa and the Zeckendorffs out of Tucson; and the Miller brothers out of Prescott. Their influence on the settlement of the West was immeasurable. As one historian has declared, "Important and spectacular as was the service of the stage-coach and the pony express in carrying the mails, a service more vital to the existence of the Indian agencies, the military posts, and the settlement in the plains and mountain regions [and he could have added the deserts and mountains of the Arizona Territory] was that rendered by the prosaic, slow-moving freight wagons."

The early merchants met many of the consumer needs of the newly-settled Salt River Valley. Barnett and Block advertised:

Dealers In
Groceries, Provisions, Clothing, Dry Goods
Wickenburg and Phoenix
Sell cheaper than any other merchants in Central Arizona

In early 1873, the *Arizona Miner* reported that Wormser and Wertheimer had just opened a store in Phoenix and "have received several barrels and casks of wines and liquors here and will soon receive several wagon loads of fresh staple goods which will be spread out for sale in their new adobe store."

The 1872 "Day Book" of J. Goldwater and Brothers of Ehrenburg provides another description of goods sold to one of their primary customers in Phoenix, Barnett and Block. In May, they filled an order in the amount of $2960 for pants, socks, overalls, calico shirts, overshirts, yards of linen, red flannel damask towels, Russian towels, combs, hats, drawers, ladies garters, woolen shawls, boots, rope, candles and food stuffs, such as sugar, bacon, oysters, canned fruit and peaches. Tea and claret were also shipped with the order. Two months later, Barnett and Block placed an order for $636 of goods, consisting of sugar, bacon, lard, soap, candles, beans, sardines, cartridges, matches, salt, string beans, peaches, tomatoes, wool socks and tea.

In May of 1878, the *Territorial Expositor* provided a rather detailed profile of the Townsite and its businesses. General merchandise stores predominated, all concentrated along Washington Street. "We count 15 general mercantile establishments in this town, great and small, about six of which carry stock well up in the tens of thousands." By 1881, a new cadre of merchants had risen to the top. The largest mercantile houses in terms of taxable inventory valuation were Goldman and Company, J. A. R. Irvine and Company (son of Edward), Nathan Rosenthal, Gus Ellis and Company, and Asher Brothers. Henry Morgan, George Loring, Woodhead and Gay and George Coats were of a lesser scale at that time. The absence of the Goldbergs in the tax valuation records and the 1882 Business Directory is curious. The Goldwaters had moved their flagship store to Prescott in 1876.

The Goldmans, who had been in business since 1874 in Phoenix, under the guidance of Adolph, first started in the vacated Heyman Menassee building. By 1880, Adolph had sold out his business interests to brother Charles, and Adolph returned to native Bavaria. Soon joined by his brother, Leo, Charles Goldman bought the larger and better-positioned Peralta building at Washington and Central.

Goldman Store

Briefly examining advertisements at that time provides a look at the range of goods offered. In March of 1878 Goldmans carried an eye-catching poetic ad:

> If you're running out of crop
> And your credit did not stop
> Go to Goldman's.
> If you prospect in the hills
> Need some powder, fuse or drills
> Go to Goldman's.

If you want some farming tools
Or some shoes for horses, mules,
        Go to Goldman's.
If there's anything in fact
By my readers lacked
From an anchor to a pin
Remember my doctrine,
        Go to Goldman's.

A later ad from Goldmans was written in a similar style:

GO TO GOLDMAN'S
If you want to buy provision
Or your Larder needs addition
        Go to Goldman's
If you need a summer suit
Or a hat or shoe or boot
        Go to Goldman's
If you want some Yankee notions
Or your girl is fond of lotions
        Go to Goldman's
If you need a pan or bucket
Or if your door you want to lock it
        Go to Goldman's

In 1879, the Goldmans ran an ad covering one full column on the front page of the *Phoenix Daily Herald* offering ladies apparel, "Gents and boys winter clothing," mattresses, pillows and comforters, parlor and cook stoves, chairs, carpet, wall paper, window shades; and "Nice things to eat," including fresh cranberries, California cornmeal, Eastern codfish, California cream cheese and Ghirardelli's chocolate.

Irvine reminded customers that "we would not be undersold in Phoenix." Irvine built a brick, 2-story building with a cellar in 1878 at Washington and 1st Street, estimated to hold $100,000 worth of goods at any one time. George Loring advertised as "the cheapest and best tobacco house in Arizona," as well as maintaining its core "news depot and stationary." In 1879, Loring installed an Italian marble soda fountain, with 18 types of syrup, three kinds of mineral water and "good old time ginger beer." Rosenthal offered "ready made clothing," as well as shoes, boots, hats, trunks and valises, and tobacco and cigars. George Coats, who arrived in 1879, advertised trees and flowers and garden seeds but also butter, honey, lard, canned goods and eggs and fruit from California. Peralta offered in 1879 the "celebrated White Sewing Machine."

Phoenix Herald

All of this advertising was possible because of the arrival of Phoenix's first newspaper. In January of 1878, Charles McClintock, the editor of the new *Salt River Herald* would write: "We have started this paper and printing enterprise in Phoenix because of the great faith we have in the general outcome of this section of the country ... coming tide of growth and prosperity ... There is no spot within the Territory of Arizona more full of promise of rapid and substantial growth than the Salt River Valley." The *Herald* was soon joined briefly by the *Territorial Expositor.*

The discerning shopper might also procure some other unusual items advertised in these newspapers: Tolu Rock and Rye was a product for "family use," a beverage with a good deal of whisky for coughs, colds and sore throats; Hostettler's "celebrated stomach bitters" (known as a "nostrum," it was 47 percent alcohol, or 94 proof); Dr. Mintle's Vital Restorative that offered cures for memory loss, "Youthful Follies," "Lost Manhood," "Nervous Debility," "aversion to society", "noise in the head," and "many other diseases that lead to insanity and death;" as well as Horne's Electro-Magnetic Medicinal Belt that promised to cure rheumatism, gout, asthma, heart disease, "sexual weakness" and impotency. A Phoenix shopper could also buy the Montgomery Ward catalog, which by 1883 had grown to 240 pages and 10,000 items.

In the mid-1870s, two other merchants discovered opportunity in the Phoenix market. Hyman Goldberg arrived in the Arizona Territory in 1862 by wagon train to Yuma on his way to Philadelphia. He stayed, establishing a general store, restaurant and saloon, a small hotel and even a freight line. His success led to his election to the 8th Arizona Territorial Legislature in 1875. But in 1876, he opened Goldberg and Sons in Phoenix that also served as a bank for local settlers. Hyman was married to a Drachman, the merchant family of Tucson. His sons, David and Aaron, would later lead the mercantile business into the 20th century, eventually merging into Hanny's, a prominent store in downtown Phoenix and Scottsdale in the 1950s and 1960s.

George H. N. Luhrs had also made his way from Prussia, embarking on his journey from Hamburg in 1867. Luhrs began working in wagon repair for the stage line in Wickenburg in 1870. He and his colleague, Newell Herrick (a blacksmith) moved to Phoenix in 1878. Luhrs was buying land in the Townsite within a year, including the 1881 purchase of Block 64 on Jefferson Street, where Luhrs and Herrick would operate the Commercial Corral. Interestingly, George listed himself as a saloon keeper in the 1880 Census. His successful hotel and real estate business would come later.

Not surprisingly, there were numerous saloons throughout the frontier era. "In the way of saloons and beer houses Phoenix is quite up to most frontier towns. We counted thirteen of these establishments and may have missed one or two," reported the *Territorial Expositor* in 1879. This count is similar to the one reported a year earlier. While there was turnover, the most popular saloons were also still located along Washington Street - the Palace, Arcade Brewery, the Magnolia Saloon (a new saloon in an old location, the Capitol Building) and others run by well-known saloon keepers such Thomas Brown, Patterson Walters, Johnny LeBarr, former Sheriff Thomas Barnum, Stephen Daneri, and Ira Stroud. While there were likely others, one Mexican operated a saloon with an Anglo partner, Haeffner and Garcia. There were two breweries, one operated by Charles Luke and Joseph Thalheimer at the Arcade Brewery and the other by Michael Wurch of the St. Louis Brewery. A John Dall operated a wholesale liquor business as did the ever-popular Johnny George.

David and Luz Balsz

And there were still bakers and butchers, again all on Washington Street. Balsz and Kelly had a butcher shop, as well as their own slaughterhouse. David Balsz had an interesting journey. Born in 1836 in Germany, his original name was David Froank. In 1884, he emigrated to St. Louis, Missouri. Trained as a butcher, Froank later went to California in the 1850s. In 1864 he arrived in Yuma and worked for Louis Jaeger, the well-known ferryman and freighter. In the 1870s Froank partnered with J. M. Redondo in founding the Yuma Exchange, a successful travelers' rest stop that included a billiard saloon, lodging house and livery stable. In 1875, by an act of the Territorial Legislature, he changed his name to David Balsz. A year later, he married his partner's daughter, Luz Redondo.

In 1878-1879, Balsz began a major cattle operation in Maricopa County with a ranch he had purchased from Fowler and the Starar brothers. This led to his partnership with John Kelly, a cattle dealer from Oakland, California. Their headquarters was four miles north of the Phoenix Townsite, with separate corrals for sheep, cattle and hogs. The two opened the butcher shop at the corner of Washington and Central in 1879. Balsz purchased the George Buck homestead in 1882 for $6,000, naming it Alameda Ranch. He transformed himself into a farmer with 1300 fruit trees and acreage in alfalfa and barley. He remained an entrepreneur for the balance of his life. He moved back to Yuma in the late 1890s, where he passed away in 1904.

Jacob Heinsohn and Carl Scherer ran their own bakeries. Sam King, Chinese, ran a bakery. There were several restaurants in town. Two of those were in the Phoenix Hotel and the Bank Exchange Hotel. An 1879 story in the *Phoenix Daily Herald* reported that there were three Chinese restaurants on Washington Street. One of these was run by Kong Lee, another by Chung Hi. Several Chinese, including Sam Wing, also ran laundries. An 1879 newspaper even referred to a "Wash House Row." Chung Sing was a "dealer in general merchandise" as were Kee Sing, offering "China goods," and Wing An Lung. The latter Chinese businessman, in 1880, loaned gardener, Ung Pung Hag, $72.70. The loan was secured by a mortgage on the following property: "one hundred chickens, 1 plow 1 horse 1 house situated upon the land ... and cultivated as a garden." It also included the existing lease with H. H. Linville and "all the crop now growing on the land." Not only did Wing An Lung have some capital, he also had quickly learned to protect his investment in this new land with a recorded mortgage. Both signed the document with their marks.

John J. Gardiner had built the first hotel in 1872 in the Phoenix Townsite, known as the Phoenix Hotel, at Washington and 3rd Streets. The original one-story adobe building was constructed in the form of a hollow square with a swimming pool, covered with a canvas canopy, in the center. It was fed by a ditch running along the west side of Third Street, with the overflow connecting to the Washington Street

Phoenix Hotel

ditch. In 1880, the Phoenix Hotel advertised "cool and elegantly furnished rooms."

One block to the east of the Phoenix Hotel a heartily-welcomed new business arrived on Washington Street in 1879 - an ice plant. Samuel Lount was the inventor of Arizona's first ice-making machine. Ammonia, shipped from San Francisco, was circulated through pipes submerged in water tanks. The capacity of the plant was one-half ton per day. Samuel started out delivering the ice door-to-door in a wheel barrow. Not surprisingly, saloons were his early and best customers.

By this time, Emil Ganz from Germany had made his way to Phoenix and in 1879 acquired a 2-story brick structure, with a veranda the width of the building, operating as the Bank Exchange Hotel. Rooms could even be reserved by telegraph and the hotel carried "only the finest liquors and cigars." Rooms ranged from $2 to $2.50 a day. That same year, Martin Kales opened the branch of his Prescott-based Bank of Arizona in Phoenix with his partner, Solomon Lewis. A brick pavement, the first of its kind, was installed in front of their bank on Washington Street.

Bank Exchange Hotel

There were, of course, a number of professional offices on Washington Street, including several lawyers and doctor offices. The former included Albert Baker, P. J. Bolan, John Rush, Joseph Campbell, Frank Cox and John Alsap. A. D. Lemon partnered with J. D. McCabe and William Hancock was a partner with Charles Tweed. Judge DeForest Porter also had an office. Dr. Thibodo still operated his practice on Washington Street. More recent medical newcomers included R. L. Rosson, Wharton and Sheets, B. L. Conyers, J. B. Farrington and Mrs. N. A. Pickens, homeopathic physician, located on Washington Street, east of the Phoenix Hotel with "Specialty: Obstetrics and Diseases of Women."

While just a block off Washington Street, George Rothrock established the first photographic studio in 1876, building a 10 by 12 foot frame house on the south side of Adams Street, between Central Avenue and 1st Street. Having recently arrived from California with his partner, William Young, the two were just getting started when Young died unexpectedly in November of 1876. Writing to Young's wife, Rothrock described the meager nature of his financial condition - "I am quite a stranger here myself. When I came here a few weeks ago, we had scarce money enough to pay my freight bill ... There are some accounts outstanding ... that he [Young] did photo work for a man to do some plowing, another for pigs, another for lumber, tools, etc - all of which might have been collected and been useful had he lived but I have not a dollar to pay expenses. I therefore propose to use [the photographic] apparatus & chemicals, stock, etc. until I can make enough to buy them as I am dependent upon them for my living, and it is my desire to do as well for you as I can."

Rothrock Photo/Washington Street

Mexican businesses were also on Washington Street. Along with Peralta, Miguel Castenada competed in this market, having moved his store from Signal City to Phoenix opposite the Plaza in 1879. Miguel Pesquiera was a well-known tinsmith, and Alberto Valencia operated a grocery store near Monroe and 1st Streets. R. G. Gonzalez, a house and sign painter, worked out of his store and home on 1st Street.

Valencia Grocery

Many of these same merchants lived at their own place of business. (A trend had just begun by 1880 to build a separate private residence on Monroe or Adams Streets. This gathered steam by the mid-1880s as old homesteads just outside the original Townsite were developed into the first residential subdivisions of Phoenix.) Individual saloon keepers as well as those with families lived behind their business. Dr. Wharton lived in a dwelling on Washington Street with his wife and six children. Dr. Rosson lived next door with an Irish miner. Darrell Duppa lived with a blacksmith and miner next to Emil Ganz' hotel, where Emil, his two Chinese cooks, two barkeepers and two boarders lived. Hyman Goldberg was next door with his store and his wife and three children, two of whom, Aaron and Dave, worked in the store. Adolph Asher (of Asher and Ellis mercantile store) lived on the store property with his brother, Morris. Nathan Rosenthal, another merchant, lived on Washington Street, with a 15 year old clerk. Next door, Henry Morgan also lived at his store with his clerk. The Lorings and Coats merchant families lived behind their stores, as well.

Homesteader farmers and a growing array of tradesmen and laborers and all of their families provided the increased demand; the merchants provided the supply. The Phoenix Townsite had become a center of trade, communication, transportation and banking. As the Disturnell Arizona Business Directory of 1881 noted - "The stores contain large stocks of merchandise and fancy ware, and carry on a profitable trade, made secure by the surrounding country." The merchants of Washington Street contributed in a significant way to this progress of civilization in the Arizona Territory.

CHAPTER SIX
A Frontier Love Story

George Loring was one of those Washington Street merchants. His journey to Arizona was precipitated by economic events in his native Massachusetts. This is his story.

Another cold blustery day hung over Marblehead, Massachusetts in the winter of 1875-76. The Panic of 1873 and its aftermath still gripped the national economy. Newspaper articles throughout the balance of the decade referred to "hard times" and "depression."

Relative newly-weds, George Loring (age 22) and his wife, Aggie (age 23), had been wed in Boston in July of 1874. Aggie was with child that winter. George had opened a watch store in Marblehead at 141 Washington Street. He also dealt in ware, spectacles and "fancy goods." His advertisement declared, "Watchmaker and Dealer in Foreign and Domestic Watches, Clocks and Jewelry ... Hair jewelry made to order."

The problem was that his small business was struggling. As he observed in a letter to his brother, Frank, "there was little money in circulation," while a later letter added, "the workmen have not had work for six or seven months and they are all on a strike." George wrote his mother, Elizabeth, early in 1875 that "Business is awful dull. I think I can do a good deal better in some other town."

Later, in November of 1875, his mother wrote to Frank that "George has got an Arizona fever." The family had conflicting opinions on this potential adventure. Father Samuel "thinks it may be a good chance for him. If he stays five years he can have 160 acres of land [certainly referring to the potential for homesteading in the Territory] and a town lot and 20 acres of mining land." Sister Annie (who was age 19 at the time) was not so convinced - "George came up [to Boston] Wednesday to the Arizona meeting ... I think George is so foolish to go to that desolate country, of which he really knows nothing ... George ought to stay home with his wife ... and not risk his life for riches which I think it extremely doubtful that he will find there."

George had indeed become convinced that the "Arizona movement ... is the best move I can make ... whether right or not, time will only tell." *The Boston Daily Globe* had been carrying stories about Arizona and the Boston lectures of former Tucson Judge, Samuel Wentworth Cozzens. His 500-plus page book, The Marvellous Country, telling stories of his travels to New Mexico and Arizona in the late 1850s, was published in 1873 in Boston. The book, itself, was not the promotional piece the title would suggest. Cozzens' vignettes centered on the area's "strange and wonderful history" and the adventures and characters he encountered along the way. He did laud that "Arizona is the most marvellous portion of this wonderful country in America." He was enamored with its "wonderful scenery," "vast canyons," "mighty rivers," and "beautiful valleys" [Albeit he did not visit the Salinas River, or Salt River, as it would become known].

George Loring

Cozzens spoke at one meeting, "conceding that much of the land is desert, [Cozzens] asserted that in the section where it is proposed to settle [northeast Arizona along the Little Colorado River], the greatest advantage as to soil, climate, lumber, water and proximity to mineral wealth are secured." Another story in the *Globe* carried the headline, "The

Promised Land." George had noted in a letter to Frank that he had also found the writings of J. Ross Browne to be "very interesting." [Browne's book, Adventures in the Apache Country was re-printed in 1871.]

George signed up with the Arizona Colonization Company (Samuel Cozzens, President), that became known in Arizona Territorial history as the Boston Colony. Certainly, he had trepidations -- "How I hate to leave her [Aggie] or the Rest of my family. I have everything to stay for in one respect and everything to go for in another." Having sold his store inventory and household goods, George left for New York and the train west in late February of 1876 with the first group of the Boston Colony. The 50 men had different motivations -- "some of them intend to try farming, others stock raising and many will devote themselves entirely to mining," reported the *Globe.*

The journey (described in several letters to his family) was both arduous and disappointing. The Mormons had already settled along the Little Colorado and at the future site of Flagstaff, this first wave of the Boston Colony dissolved. George and some others went down to Prescott, the Territorial capital. A few months later, only five remained as the rest had journeyed on to California. A letter in the *Boston Herald* in June, written by several members of this first party, denounced the "Cozzens enterprise as a humbug and swindle." But not before the second party of the Boston Colony had already departed for the Arizona Territory.

This had been a difficult time for George. He missed Aggie deeply, compounded by not being present at the birth of their first child, George, in February, 1876. George wrote to Aggie from Prescott, trying to console her concerns over their future -- "Do not feel disappointed because the Colony was not a success. I think I can find a place a good deal better than that would have been." But then he added that "Prescott is over-run with watchmakers." A letter in late June poured out his feelings for his wife: "my whole happiness is centered on my precious wife, all the riches that this world could give me would not be one drop compaired with the happiness my darling gives me."

[Excerpts from the Loring family letters are transcribed from the original, with spelling and grammatical errors.]

In turn, Aggie tried to remain stoic and resolute. Her letters generally focused on baby "Georgie" and other family members. But her heart still ached for her husband. "I try to be happy and make the best of everything ... But, oh, I miss you more and more and I long to be with you ... I know you are doing what is for the best but I feel lonely sometimes. it seems as though I could not endure to be separated from you any longer and then I think of the trials and dangers you are exposed to and I feel if God will only spare your life, I will be content."

The summer of 1876 held more adventures for George Loring. In a letter to Aggie on July 9, he was concerned that his "cash is running very low." He was heading to Phoenix to examine prospects there, catching a wagon ride with a Mexican. They camped the first night at Virgin Mary's ranch but "she was not a virgin by any means," George noted. On to Big Bug Canyon, down Black Canyon and across the desert -- "the desert was I supposed like all deserts, barren, sandy and hot." Their mules ran off and George finished part of the trek on foot.

"I had on a flannel shirt so felt the heat very much. their are some beautiful ranches ... I think most any thing can be raised here. I saw some fine crops as I came in and peach trees ... Diches run all over the land, it all has to be irrigated. the land is level. the streets are laid out in squares. on each side of the street there are diches from Salt River. the dogs and horses drink from it . Mexican women use it to wash in, in fact it is used for everything. there are wells here in which the water is much better ... Cotton wood trees have been planted close together all along the diches. Which gives the street a good appearance. The houses are made of adobe. I have not seen many white women here. they say their is quite a number here."

"Their are quite a number of Indians here. they are coming and going from the reservation all the time. some of the braves wear nothing but a shirt. the squaws wear a piece of calico pinning tight around their loins and a chimizi short, hanging loose. Most of them have a half-breed young one with them."

In Phoenix, George "hired a hut" to share with an Irish shoemaker from Prescott. He seemed pleased with the early results of his watch repair business but wanted to look into the Florence market. "I think now I have got where I can make some money, and if you don't raise that courage of yours, I shall give you a fearful scolding," he wrote to Aggie. During these same early days in Phoenix, George wrote to his father that he "had commenced business here on a small scale." He wrote now the first of many letters to his family back in Boston requesting inventory for his work -- different sizes of watch glasses, bench key, screw driver, drills, and a "Shamie Skin." "Tell Mother she need not send the flannel shirt but send me a pair of linen pants and my linen shirt. You have no idea how hot it is here." George noted that with a large Mexican population, he needed a Spanish dictionary. "The candle is nearly out ... so I must close."

George continued to express to Aggie his commitment, his "duty" to "stay here in the Territory ... I have got a living to make for us. and money to make for Geo education, and for a rainy day, and when we are aged and gray ... If I stay here I am shure of making money ... You have been a brave patient darling ... keep up your courage and I will do the best I can for Aggie and our baby boy. my life and everything I do is for them ... O darling, it is awful hard to be out here away from you and our little blessing ... I could not stand it to be separated if I did not think I was doing my duty. I have got a home to earn, and there is no prospect in the East to get ahead but I can work into a business here ... every cent I save will bring my Aggie to me sooner."

George described his cabin to Aggie -- "I have a little fire place in one corner where I backe my bread and do my working. I have my wagon covering down for a carpet, and have rigged me up a bench and made me a stool. the sun strikes all over the cabin so makes it very warm."

Prospects in Phoenix were not improving, as George noted in his letter to his Mother in late July of 1876. He had been forced to seek new quarters, a fact he had not shared with Aggie. "I had to take a little old played out dirty, buggy rough little old Harness shop. their was a hole where the window should have been ... the first thing I done was to shovel the place out

... made me a shutter to put up to the square hole." George put that same wagon covering down for his carpet and put his luggage in one corner of the room. " I have to pay five dollars a month for it."

"I have got to connect something else with the repairing. If I could have a shop and keep a stock little of everything I could make lots of money, land don't cost much here and a dobie house can be put up cheap. I know I could make money if I could get a start ... A man could make money here ranching. a man could make a fortune raising hogs." George was clearly mulling over his options.

George then related to his mother how much he missed his wife. "I do not want to live without Aggie and the baby. I am ready to go through any thing, deprive myself of any thing and work as hard as I can stand and live any whays, if I can live with my Dear Wife and child but I cannot go many long without them. I don't know but this climate would be to hot for Aggie. if it is I don't want any part of it. I shall not live where she cannot ... she might stand the three summer months, the rest of the year is delightful." He must have been concerned that his letters were perhaps compelling family members to encourage Aggie to wait until prospects improve.

A day later he wrote a similar letter to Aggie, wondering if she would rather stay in Boston. "I guess you would not like to live in a mud house, cook in a fire place, give up good things to eat, sleep on a hard bed, be deprived of society and most everything that civilization makes pleasant. you would have to put up with lots of inconvenientuntces. And in return you would only have your husband's Love ... do you think you can enjoy life more here with me or in Boston with friends, and everything to make life happy." George's portrayal of life in Phoenix was not complimentary; nor did it present an enticing option to Boston society. He certainly deserved credit for some brutal honesty.

August arrived with some additional opportunities for George; he made friends with merchant, Adolph Goldman. He not only was offered a window in Goldman's store but also a little room in the back to sleep in (when he wasn't sleeping outside or in his harness shop/ adobe). Goldman would be traveling to San Francisco in September and had asked George to manage the store in his absence. "I want to get an insight into the business here, they keep a little of everything in their store here. I want to get posted on the buying and selling prices as I may want to go in to the same business myself." He also thought he might even open up a restaurant and lodging house.

George acknowledged "it will take time, patience and denial" to become a "rich man ... but I have started out for my fortune, and it is not going to be my fault if I do not earn it. You do not know how much I want Aggie to be with me. It don't seem right to have my smart little boy grow up without me even in his infant days. It is worth a fortune to me to be with him. I must wait and be patient. And God in his own good time will bring us togeather."

A "Heathen Chinese" had recently come in the store to get a watch repaired; George charged $8 dollars. "Somehow I cannot charge as much as I ought to. I don't even know what they think their watches are worth. I am afraid that they will think it cheaper to throw their watches away and buy another." George later related to his mother that his intention was to open a "News Depot and Stationary and Variety Shop." George was committed to Phoenix, with some misgivings -- "Now I have started in, I want to carry it out ... Knowing as much as I do now, I should have choosed home [Boston]."

George was looking at lots in the Phoenix Townsite for "putting up a store and house." He was looking at lots [likely he meant blocks] 41, 42 or 43 because rents were so high. He also had plans to travel to Florence and Ft. McDowell to seek out watch repair business.

On those occasions of travel, George wore a vest. "I have to use it for a safe. I cannot leave any Watches in my hut, so have to carry them in my vest arond with me I have quite a variety of watch guard attached to me. could not have got along with out the Shirts, vest, knife, and oil."

George was also thankful for papers and magazines sent from home. In August, he wrote to his mother thanking her for the batch of cookies that had just arrived in the mail from Prescott. "The cookies will taste good ... When I eat them I shall think of the kind hands and heart that prepaired and sent them." Then George inexplicably wrote, "wish you had not sent them. would rather have had the weight in some thing I can turn for the all mighty Dollar." George was doggedly focused on making a living in the Territory. "I am not earning a great deal," he wrote in the same letter, "still I am saving something every day."

In a lengthy letter to brother Frank in August, 1876, George related a number of stories that provide a glimpse into life in frontier Phoenix. First, and foremost, the summer heat certainly warranted a spirited tale. "You ask how the weather is in Arizona. that is a hard question to answer. there is all kinds of climate from San Fr mts [San Francisco Mountains in the area of the place destined to be called Flagstaff] to the east. But I will tell you as near as I can what the weather is here in Phoenix Sweat-vill."

"If a man get up at three oclock am and sits perfectly still in some open spot (where he can get the advantage of what breeze there is) without a rag on. he can be comfortable. the sweat will not run, but understanding, he has got to keep perfectly still. if he moves his toes they will be covered with persperation. he must not wink more than once in fifteen minutes. if he speaks the sweat will ooze out of his neck as if it will filled with water and covered with only a cloth strainer. if he thinks hard the sweat will come out all over his head. If a man will stick to the above rules he can keep middling comfortable for just one hour. and then it begins to grow warm, hot, scorching, heating, red hot, no <u>white hot</u>. the men never wear coats or vests here. thin pants and cotton shirt. you walk ten steps in the sun here, and you will perspire more than any race horse after he has trotted his mile heat ... It is a serious thing here to joke a man in the middle of the day. a good laugh in the hot of the day here would over heat a man blood so as to cause his death. The thermer__ goes up to 108 in the shade with out a breath of air and I don't think the things works right. I think it is nearer 150 degrees."

"No one here sleeps in the house. they all have their wooden beds out doors behind the houses and shops. some have them on the sidewalk and a good many sleep on the sidewalks without boards made in the shape of a bedstead. You take a walk in the morning and you would have to turn out often to go round Mexican women and men sleeping on the sidewalk. the above will give you som idea of the climate, at this time of year. in the winter they say it is delightful from the middle of September until June." Later on, George concedes that "I can stand the weather first rate and hope it will not abuse me."

In the same letter, written over several days, George also experienced a monsoon storm. "Last night I was awoke by rain drops gently pattering over me. I lost no time in rolling up blankets took up my bed and run. I was dressed very loose. I had on my hat and slippers. After reaching my mud house the rain came down in torrents. the whole sky would lighten up by the continual lighteng. the thunder was tremendous. the wind blew a perfect gale tearing limbs from the cotton woods. it took the part of the roof of from my German friends store house ... It would take a Doz Boston storm combined in one, to mach one of these."

He wrote later in the letter that sleeping outside could even be dangerous. "It is sometimes unpleasant here nights as some of the boys have a way of amusing them selves nights when a little inhaled, By walking around and shooting at persons feet ... To see how near they can shoot without hitting. They mean no harm. A fellow said the other night a ball whizzed over his shoulder and then another just grazed his toe. He thought the best thing he could do would be to light out, so he lighted."

George provided some of his views on Phoenix for his brother. "The town of Phoenix is in a large valley ... the town depends altogeather on the ranches for support, I think most any thing can be raised here. though wheat and barley is the principal crop. all the land ... is irrigated from the Sault River. all the water here has a sault taste. they raise very good peaches and grapes here. But the ranchmen have no ambition. all they care for is to get enough to eat and rum enough to drink ... the houses are all dobie, which make a cheap comfortable house. the Town is laid off in squars with good wide streets, a dich from the main dich running on each side with cotten wood trees close togeather on the side of the dich. it gives the street a very good appearance." George had witnessed all kinds of diversion and entertainment in his short time in Phoenix. "Night before last a man influenced by Phoenix rum called a bar keeper one of those names that reflects badly on one of his parents. The Gentleman of the bar lost no time in putting the back of his hand on the back of the man's neck, in such a way as to cause the man to drop never to rize again. A jury was summoned. They gave in a verdict that the afore said man died from the cause of heat and rum."

George had heard there was a good band at the "post" [Fort McDowell] but he had not yet seen them. "The Band stand [in town] is occupied nightly by all drunks ... I have been told that they have religious services here ... I guess I will hunt the church up. It will kinder please the Old Women, I mean Aggie. I have been to the school house (used for a meeting house) found it closed. I reckon the minister is on a drunk." George evidently witnessed a good deal of drinking around town. At that time there were perhaps six to ten saloons from which to choose.

His letter to his mother of August 20 was quite optimistic. "I do wish so that Aggie could come out this fall. she will have nine months of the pleasantest weather in the W. States ... This is the best locality in Arizona and at some future clime will be thickly settled if the mines are developed ... tell father if he was younger we would do a smashing big business here. we would get rich rich rich. How good it sounds."

In September, 1876 George was making plans for Aggie and Georgie's upcoming trip to Phoenix. He reported to Aggie that "Florence is not as pretty a place as Phoenix. the streets are narrow and diches crossing the street everywhere ... their is not so many white people here ... I think Phoenix will be the largest place in time."

George's letters in September were still centered on convincing his mother that Aggie's move to Phoenix was for the best. His journal and letters describing his trip to Arizona and even his views on the conditions in Phoenix had caused her much consternation. George's descriptions of the summer, and his difficulties in getting work, were worrisome. "It is true that was a miserable night to me when I arrived here. their was a feeling come over me that I can never forget. no one can know what it is until they have experienced it. I vowed that for my boy would never let a friendless and homeles person go without help. But their it is all over. I am comfortable situated and it made me better."

George goes on to address the weather. "from the middle of May to the middle of September, the weather is hot as in all warm climates ... After the middle of Sep fine weather commences to come in ... I don't think the summer here is more unhealthy than Boston is in the winter ... Prescott is within visiting distance they could go their if necessary ... And without a doubt I could make arrangements for Aggie to go on to some good white man's ranch in Prescott in the summer."

He reassured his mother later that month that "their is no Territory or state in the U S that will touch Arizona to make money in. Any business man with Capital and business ability and capital can make a fortune here ... but mind you it is no baby play to come in to this country and begin life and business. a man has got to endure hardships and be made of good grit."

By that time, Aggie and young Georgie had already departed for Arizona; the *Chronicle* announcing their arrival in San Francisco on September 22, 1876. Aggie's loneliness, George's appeals, and their love for each other had overcome the ever-present reservations. In one of her first letters to her family a few weeks later from Phoenix, Aggie related that "We are having beautiful weather here now. so warm that I washed out at the back door and I tied baby up in a high chair beside the tub ... We have got two goats and I give him [Georgie] all the milk he will drink ... Geo thinks he is beautiful."

In November, she sent her own description of life in Phoenix. "Our house and store are in one building on Washington Street in the center of town. and I have one room. I have a carpet chairs table and bed. table clothes, napkins towels sheets and pillow slips. I have got my bed dressed in white ... I find the place much pleasanter than I expected. Geo gave me the very worse side of the story. I have got so I can cook over the fire place nicely ... I make cakes pies bread and you can get every kind of canned fruit fish meat ... We can get nice sweet potatoes that are raised here but nearly all the Irish potatoes and vegetables come from Prescott ... We have got nine hens and a rooster ... I am going to sell all the eggs I can ... I have got some real nice neighbors Yankees that live across the St. We have a Literary Association ... they have decided to have the library in our store and have chosen me for librarian ... George stays at home and takes care of baby so I can go to Church. Saturday evening we take him with us [to Literary Association meetings; Aggie was active with this group and in creating the library that would soon boast of having 250 books] ... George is going to keep a variety store ... and I shall make cakes and pies to sell." Aggie noted that "if nothing happens it will be but a little while before I shall be home again." Aggie must have felt this was temporary until George made his fortune.

In a letter to her brother-in-law Frank, Aggie described her rather sparse furnishings -- "my chairs are roughly made with raw hide ... One room has carpet, one has a dirt floor ... Mr. Larkin [George's first real friend and sometime business associate] has a very good room, plastered and a good board floor, two windows and 2 doors, one opens on to the St ... and the other into the kitchen." Aggie can use the room if she gets a "good bedstead bureau and wash stand ... And with the lounge my rocking chair and a chair Mr. Stearns [another merchant in town] I can have a nice little room and all I shall want as long as I stay here." She wore her silk dress to a recent party, "It was the most stylish dress thare."

At the end of 1876, George's father wrote, "I feel quite hopeful as to your future -- industry, economy and perseverance, coupled with honesty, must eventually work out a success." These quintessential American attitudes had certainly been passed down to George and had provided him, as well as Aggie, the resolute courage and strength for this journey.

Loring's Bazar

1877 started out be a good year for George's variety store, Lorings Bazar [as the photo depicts, George chose to spell it "Bazar"]. Aggie wrote to her parents that "1.00 was the highest price for candy and .75 the lowest price. We sell about 100 pounds a month. A clock that cost George 2.5 in the East he sells here for 8.00 dollars ... George has sent to San Francisco for a supply of oranges, Lemons figs pears and all kinds of nuts ... this summer he will keep peaches, grapes and all kinds of fruit." They expected the Post Office to open in their store that April. "George works very hard. Saves every cent & I think it will be a little while before we can go home." For extra cash, the Lorings had taken in a boarder for a few weeks; he paid $7.00 dollars a week, receiving breakfast and a 4:00 p.m. dinner. Aggie even had a nine-year old Indian girl helping her for a time with daily chores and watching Georgie.

Aggie appeared to enjoy the desert in Spring. "The weather is lovely now. the trees are all leaved out. the farmers have got their grain in and it is coming up and in about four months they will commence to harvest."

The Spring of 1877 also brought news of tragedy. Aggie was saddened (a "fearful blow") to hear of her brother Charlie's death in Iowa. "Now the family circle is broken and little do we know who will be taken next."

Phoenix was still a small but growing adobe town, a farming community, in 1878. The *San Francisco Herald* proclaimed the Salt River Valley to be "a land of fertility and sunshine. The green foliage on the cottonwood and other trees, the thousands of acres of wheat and barley already shading the earth, gardens and vegetables, etc. reminded us of May in Kansas." The town's growing population added to the optimism.

George Loring's Bazar, located on the south side of Washington Street, was in an enviable location. It was just two doors down from the Maricopa County Courthouse. The store not only housed the Post Office but also Wells Fargo, making it the location for the stagecoaches coming into town as well as for the Telegraph Office.

Loring's adobe store and dwelling in the rear was the third building built in the Phoenix Townsite, originally constructed by Johnny George. He later sold it to William Bichard who ran a store and flour business until perhaps 1875. By 1878, George had moved into the vacant building, without permission of the Bichard heirs. He repaired the building and had its outside walls plastered.

Loring's advertisement in the *Salt River Herald* called it a "News Depot," with fruits, candy, nuts, stationary, blank books and school books, jewelry, silverware, watches and clocks. "Smokers made happy at the News Depot." In addition, George and his friend, Matt Larkin, similar to other early pioneers, had taken out the "Yankee" mining claim up in the Cave Creek Mining District in early March of 1878. With a degree of good cheer, Aggie wrote home in February that George "is doing very good business ... And the place [Phoenix] is growing every year."

Most importantly, in the lives of George and Aggie Loring, Aggie was pregnant. Surprisingly, her letters home did not discuss her feelings about this. Aggie's March, 1878 letter home was very optimistic. She noted that the new church [United Methodist Episcopal Church, South] was nearly completed; in the meantime, "they have services in the courthouse. it is only a few steps from here. I usually go in the evenings." George's business was "doing very well ... He is obliged to take one of my rooms to enlarge his store and will put me up another one ... I shall have the nicest furnished room in town when I get my furniture ... I should like to see you all and I think I will in a little while."

Her tone was not so encouraging in mid-May. The stage had been robbed outside of Wickenburg and she was fearful her package home had been stolen. Moreover, summer was coming -- "soon it will be so hot everything will be burned up. and it will be dreary enough." She was pleased with a recent church festival and that the Issacs were going to have she and George out to their farm for the day. She related that Mrs. Loring had recently sent her a very handsome summer bonnet trimmed with black velvet and white silk and pale pink flowers. "it is turned up on one side. I have a new blue cambric & am going to have a new muslin to wear to Church." She revealed that "we have to be very saving for George says he does not want to stay in this country only five years and then we will go home again whither we have money or not ... It is so warm George will not let me do my washing so I give it to a chinaman and he washes and irons for 1.50 a week and my clothes look beautifully."

Aggie's health during her final stage of pregnancy was not good. She wrote on July 7, 1878 that "for the past month I have been sick with the neuraliga [neuralgia, a painful nerve condition] in my face and teeth." Her eating had been sporadic and she was unable to sleep without taking "sleeping powders." Aggie was compelled to have one tooth pulled and was fearful all would be removed, "but I suppose my face would look just the same." She was so excited to recently have some ice "as large as my hand ... you have no idea how nice the ice tasted."

Aggie once more turned her thoughts to home, wishing "I could sit down to your table and eat one good square meal ... I believe I never spent a more miserable day than this last Fourth of July ... and it seemed to me I must take wings and fly back and see you all and more. Only two short years have passed and Charlie has been taken from us and God only knows which one will be taken next. it may be me or may be you." Aggie ruefully complained of the summer heat, "106, 108 in the shade but I just lie around and make my self as comfortable as possible."

George added this postscript -- "The morning after Aggie wrote this at four oclock our little home was blessed with a boy babie weighing 9 ½ lbs [Madison Roby Loring]. Aggie is very well and we are very much pleased with our boy."

Tragically, Aggie was not well. That was to be her last letter home. Aggie Loring passed away on August 12, 1878 at the home of William and Lillie Hancock. She was only 25 years old. George wrote to his mother that very day with the news -- "They have taken my life away - My good Aggie! She has gone - left me forever on earth! ... Oh, my Mother. I am so lonely. what shall I do? ... I have nothing to live for now: my courage, ambition, life died this morning. Why did they take her and leave me alone! ... Now they have taken her away! What shall I do! What shall I do! Oh Mother! Can't you come out and stay with me? I don't care to stay in this world long. I want to go to Aggie! But while I am here I must work for my two darling boys ... . If you can -- no, don't you come out. they may kill you! ... Good by, dear Mother. do not worry about me, but think of me. and love me for I am alone now!"

Later that same month, another letter from George continued with his deepest sorrow. "She was my life my comfort. My aim in life was to make her and our children happy ... she had two darling boys and she loved her husband and children as only a few can love and why did God take her from her happy home and her dear dear ones." George wrote that Aggie developed a fever and it got better, then worse. "I had two of the best Doctors here who visited her for four and six hours during the twenty four and one of them set up with her." They had moved her down the street to the home of William and Lillie Hancock. Towards the end, "she could not speak only with her eyes and hold her sweet lips for me to kiss and Mrs. Hancock. the pain left her and the angels of god came to her. her face changed to a bright smile and our dear dear darling went to heaven."

In the immediate aftermath, Lillie Hancock (herself only 23) took little Georgie while her mother, Mary Kellogg, took Madison to the Kellogg farm. As she wrote to Aggie's mother, Mrs. Roby, Lillie had these consoling words to say -- "so kind, so good and gentle. always trying to make everyone around her happy. she always had a smile and a pleasant word for everyone. And all that knew her loved her. Even the poor Mexican women that she had been kind to came and threw themselves down beside her crying that their best friend was gone." Aggie "passed away very quietly like a tired child going to rest." George "poor boy he is heartbroken but tries to bear up for his children's sake."

As Lillie related in a September letter to Mrs. Roby, Aggie's decline was due to a number of circumstances. After Madison's birth, little Georgie caught a fever and Aggie became "overworked." A "fearful rain storm can in. and the roof leaking she took cold." The doctor thought she had the bilious fever [a pioneer term for fever with vomiting; also referred to as typhoid fever]. No one apparently thought her life was in danger. But the fever kept coming back. "we had her carried to our house. the weather was threatening and we thought the roof might leak ... She did not want to come for fear she might give us trouble. sick as she was she thought more about others than of her self. she slept very well till midnight. after that she was very restless. talked about you and her brothers and sisters. said several times 'don't tell Mother I am sick for she will worry so about me' ... she did not complain of any pain except her head." At one point she ate some gruel and grapes ("she had been living on Brandy and Wine whey for three or four days") and seemed as if she might be getting better.

Later in the day she started to breathe hard and the doctor put a blister on her chest [a hot plaster that caused a second degree burn that would then be drained to purportedly remove the toxin and infection] which seemed to provide relief. Later that evening "her bowels began running off ... she suffered a great deal." Later, the doctor "ordered mustard on her feet, hands, chest, etc, but in vain". [Mustard paste applied on cloth was placed on the skin to alleviate chest congestion.] George "poor boy did not know till the last that she was going ... so sudden ... more than he could bear."

The doctor reported Aggie had "Bilious fever and then she took cold and Typhoid Pneumonia set in and carried her off." All of the known pioneer remedies, practiced at random, may have actually led to Aggie's death. Lillie went on to relate that "I do not know what Mr. Loring's plans are. he hardly knows himself. I believe that he has written to his Mother to come out here to live with him." Lillie closed this sad letter with "Let us hope that we may meet in that better land to which she has gone."

On August 20, George wrote to his father that "I am feeling discouraged and homesick and heartsick ... I do not think it would be right for me to leave here. I have got to make a living for myself and children and know of no place that I can do it as well as here." He asked once again that his parents come to Arizona, for "I cannot feel right that my boys should be brought up by friends." He even requested that his father come by way of Cincinnati and meet with Nicolas Bichard to buy their property in Phoenix.

In a letter to his parents in September prior to their departure for Phoenix, George provided them advice and even some business suggestions: "take a large canteen and see that it is filled when you get on the stage and you had better take a bottle of light wine do not packages with you to be bothered with on the stage remember the stages in this country are not like the old coaches we use to have in Maine but they are narrow contracted boxes and you will not more than have room to sit it will be hard enough for you without being bothered with bundles you go to Yuma and buy a ticket their for Maricopa Wells and I will meet you their you will stop at Gila Bend Station it is owned by Mr.

Decker Mrs. Decker was Aggie's Great friend she say it seems as if She had lost her only Friend in Phoenix ... Blankets are not included with baggage and you want to take a pair of blankets you may have cool nights." George requested that his father call on a "drummer" representing Sanderson and Horn; "buy me a lot of canned goods." In Yuma he wanted his father to call on pioneer merchant David Neahr -- " I may want him to look after some Freight business." George assured them that he will try to make it "pleasant" for them in Phoenix.

Father Samuel Loring replied to his son in late September, "The loss of Aggie and your deep affliction have weighed us down ... our desire now is to do all in our power to alleviate this affliction, and, if possible, to render your home a happy one - believing as we do that there is yet prosperity and happiness in store for you in the future."

There were no more letters. The *Salt River Herald* reported on October 26, 1878 that Samuel and Elizabeth Loring had arrived and "will make Phoenix their home." Brother Frank would soon join them. Together, they began to buy real estate in the Phoenix Townsite and build a thriving business. With his family's love and support, George appeared to have recovered from this tragedy and married Jennie Clark in 1881. They had three more children together. Samuel died in Phoenix in 1888 at the age of 79.

However, by 1900, George and Jennie no longer lived together. At some point, prior to 1910, George moved to Los Angeles where he ran a grocery store for a number of years. His mother, Elizabeth, died there at age 87. Brother Frank, who had gone into business with George in Phoenix, also moved to Los Angeles where he passed away in 1930. George Loring, a successful pioneer merchant whose journey west brought such travails and tragedy, likely never forgot his first love. He passed away in February, 1936 in Los Angeles, with Aggie's last child, Madison, at his side.

CHAPTER SEVEN
Sketches of Town Life

Capturing the flavor, the rhythm of town life in frontier Phoenix is a daunting task. The lack of reminiscences and the late appearance of the local newspaper (1878) contribute to the dilemma. So, the story of frontier life is perhaps a sketch at best.

In describing everyday life in the Phoenix Townsite, it is well to remember that this was an agricultural community. The day's activities were dictated by the two growing seasons, revolving around the time of planting and of harvesting. The vast majority of settlers grew up on farms across America and in Mexico. This was certainly true with the young families that began to migrate westward after the Civil War. Owning land and pursuing farming was one early American dream that advanced westward with settlement. Hence, farm life, marriage, family, and the creation of social institutions was a natural progression within this rural outpost.

For the vast majority who were farm laborers, theirs remains an untold story. Days were long and pay was low. Then, there were trades people living in town, generally behind their place of business. Long hours, goods to be purchased and then goods to be freighted to and from Phoenix, oftentimes in trying circumstances, with Indian threats and robberies, was the bulk of their day. And in the difficult financial times of the 1870s, as evidenced by the travails of George Loring or George Rothrock, daily life might well have simply been a struggle to stay solvent.

In times like those, overshadowed by such conditions, bordering on tedium and even isolation, social connections were vital. Hence, the early arrival of the saloon, then several, then many. There is no first-hand account of saloon life and its accompanying vice of prostitution in frontier Phoenix. If George Hand's (Tucson saloon keeper) diary of the mid-1870s is an indication, the saloon certainly must have been an important influence on the largely single male culture of Phoenix. Other forms of entertainment and social interaction such as gatherings for weddings, dances, local and Territorial political elections (of which there is surprisingly little documentation or newspaper reporting), community celebrations and festivals provided a welcome opportunity to gather together. As the culture became more family-oriented and population growth created the requisite demand, Phoenix experienced the rise of churches and other institutions, from fraternal organizations to associations concerned with music, literacy and even temperance. As Phoenix reached another stage of maturity, the town became a magnet for entertainment coming to Phoenix - roving theater troupes and circus groups. The desire to engage in more participatory activities led to theater, local bands, and baseball, all in the late 1870s.

The first public activity of every fledgling community in the West was the creation of perhaps a private school, followed by a tax-supported public school. A belief in education was a paramount tenet of the American character. The Phoenix experience was no exception.

A sufficient number of families with children had arrived by August of 1870, thereby prompting the *Arizona Miner* to report: "The citizens [of the Salt River Valley] are anxious for a school, and intend to have one as soon as possible, both for their own convenience and as a strong inducement for outside families." It was not any easy task, but in early 1871, the Sixth Territorial Legislature passed a new law for the establishment of public schools. John Alsap was the first Superintendent of Schools for newly-established Maricopa County. In June of 1871, he appointed William Kirkland, James A. Young and John P. Osborn as the first trustees for School District No. 1. They were succeeded in May of 1872 at the general election by William Hancock, J. D. Rumberg, and again, John Osborn.

Alsap, however, was the driving force. In October of 1871, he wrote a letter to Governor Safford, noting it was "impossible to procure a suitable house" for the school: "Our people are busy sowing grain, Digging Ditches, and our valley is beginning to look as though the people meant to stay here ... New houses are going up in town all the time and there are no empty ones." Alsap raised concerns with raising money for books from San Francisco - "I am hardly able to pay for them myself." The County Board of Supervisors rented a room to the School District, in their adobe courthouse, located on south 1st Avenue, just off Washington Street. The *Tucson Citizen* reported in April of 1872 : "The liberality shown in maintaining free schools in Salt River Valley, is in the highest degree worthy of imitation all over the Territory, and we believe will prevail. We freely accord much credit to Judge Alsap for the splendid progress of the free school system at Phoenix, but by his own report, he showed how well the citizens there seconded all his efforts." The first permanent public school in Tucson opened in March of 1872.

J. R. "Dolph" Darroche was the first teacher in Phoenix, succeeded in October of 1872 by J. Parker, then W. A. Glover in early 1873. Early reports suggest that class size ranged from 20-25. A surviving class photo for 1872 shows 21 children. The class was dominated by the Murray girls, followed by the Kellogg, Osborn, Roberts and Kirkland

1873 Elementary School

children. The ages ranged from four or five years of age to teenagers (John Osborn was 18) and even Eli T. Hargrave at age 24. There were three Mexican children, all boys - two from the Rodriguez family and one Angel Moreno.

1873 was an important year for the School District. The first schoolhouse was constructed on the block reserved for the school by the Town Association, on the west side of Central Avenue, between Monroe and Van Buren - a 20 by 30 foot adobe with a dirt floor and a shingle roof; three windows on each side, a fireplace at one end and a double door at the entrance. It did have plaster walls. Richard Pearson made the school desks. Building material was contributed by several merchants. The School trustees at this time were J.D. Rumberg, Benjamen Patterson and George Roberts.

In addition, with the assistance of Governor Safford, the School District recruited Miss Ellen Shaver, a school teacher from Wisconsin, to be in charge of the school. At the time, she was likely paid $100 a month. But, as happened so often with newly-arrived single teachers in the West, she married John Y. T. Smith in 1875, thus requiring her to relinquish her post. Other early teachers included Mrs. Allie Greenhaw Fitzpatrick (a widow) who also left her position in 1876 after marrying homesteader and farmer John Montgomery. Carrie Hancock, the sister of William, succeeded her but moved to Sacramento, California the following year. Keeping school teachers in those early days was troublesome.

It appears that in the mid-1870s the school, operating nine months out of the year, routinely had a class size of 35-40. By 1878, the student body numbered 80, and by 1880, that number had reached 104. Surviving records of an 1874 School Census reported that only 38 students attended school out of 264 children between the ages of 6 and 21. Of the 89 Mexican families in that Census, only Jesus Otero reported sending his three children to school. Columbus Gray reported one school-age child (this would be Mary Green's African-American daughter) but she did not attend school.

With increasing population pressure, in the fall of 1880, a new, two-story brick schoolhouse, Central School, was built on that same reserved block, later referred to as the "Block of Knowledge." By this time there were three teachers. The School Board at that time was lawyer Alexander Lemon, rancher Hiram Linville and the ever-present John T. Alsap.

Central School

The other "civilizing" influence within new communities was the church. Its importance is underscored by the Town Association's donations of lots to the early churches. The church served as a gathering and social point for young families in a rather remote environment. While records are scant, it is not unusual to find early church services at homes and ranches. Jack Swilling's "Castle" was the site for early Catholic services. Otero hosted services in his home later in the 1870s, with a priest traveling from nearby Florence. The Catholic Church would later build in 1881 on Block 4 on Monroe and 3rd Streets on land donated by the Town Association, King Woolsey, Miguel Peralta, Edward Irvine, James Monihon and Carlos Perazza. Jesus Otero's family provided some furniture and icons to this first church. Vicar J. B. Salpointe spearheaded these efforts to establish a formal church.

The Methodist Episcopal Church, South (a denomination that had split off over slavery in 1844) sent out a Reverend McKean, then a Reverend Groves from California in 1871. It was recounted that "Parsons Groves held religious meetings Friday and Saturday evenings, and three separate services on Sunday in the pleasant grove on the ranch of Thomas Barnum. During the Sunday services quite a number attended from Phoenix. After morning services an impromptus table was arranged, and an excellent dinner, gotten up by Mrs. John Osborn, Mrs. Griffin, Mrs. Thomas Barnum, and Mrs. Rodgers, was served to the visitors, who did ample justice to the viands. The intervals between the services were occupied in singing and recreation. Those who lingered to the last sat down to a pleasant supper with Mrs. Barnum, and all departed much pleased with the day's proceedings." Edward Irvine recalled meeting Reverend Groves in 1872: "All along, as I went, I passed excellent farms which bore evidence of having produced abundant crops the year past, and of active preparations being made for extensive sowing during the coming season. On Hiltibrand's ranch, I surprised Parson Groves, black as a negro, busy with fork and axe, clearing off the mesquite brush. The parson works thus during the week, and preaches at Phoenix nearly every Sunday, and occasionally down at Mesquite and up at Barnum's Grove, walking backwards and forwards a distance of ten or twelve miles one way." Reverend Groves was also known to grow potatoes and vegetables and would carry his produce to the miners in the Bradshaw Mountains for barter, and do some preaching along the way.

One of the most successful church gatherings of the early days was the quarterly conference of the ME Church, South, which was held at Phoenix in the courthouse (the building constructed by Hancock and Monihon), commencing on Friday, December 5, 1873, and closing on Sunday evening. The attendance was reported to have been good in spite of the rain and mud. A Reverend Gill lectured on at the courthouse on "Theology" on Sunday evening to close out the conference. The first Church conference was held in 1872 and lasted four days. The Methodists held services in the new adobe schoolhouse by 1873 or 1874. In the mid-1870s, Reverend George "Headerbed" Herritt ("a long, lanky, fiery-haired exhorter of the Methodist persuasion") was a roving minister who would ride around and gather his congregation in a wagon that was half full of hay. He often used the wagon as his pulpit. Similar to Groves, he had to make a living; he had a contract with Edward Irvine to raise chickens on Irvine's ranch.

In July of 1876, George Loring described attending a church meeting in one of his letters to Aggie: "I went to meeting last night. It was just at dark. I could only see a large band of white in one corner of the room. I heard a voice from the white bands. I found it to be the long necked Parson [Herritt] we had quite a long chat about business. Two of the head members arrived before we got to religion. The first ½ doz. men that came brought dogs with them which made a good deal of flying round to clear the rooms then came the young ladies a man took a broom and sweep the dust off from the seats, their was seven ladies tolerable looking, don't get jealous they did not look so pretty to me as you do. Then came a couple with a baby who showed great ambition to sing when the others struck up. We shall have to take Geo to meeting with us. suppose he will keep quiet."

In 1878, the ME Church, South built a 28 by 32 foot adobe church on Monroe Street, near Central. The church was built with lumber for the floors, windows, and roof, with material from Prescott. Everything was made by hand. Their membership was only 45 but included the Alsaps, Irvines, Barnums, Grays and Osborns. A year later, the Presbyterians were to occupy the second story of a frame building on the south side of the Plaza.

It was said that frontier settlers would gather for dancing at any opportunity. Weddings often provided a natural opportunity for festivity. One such recorded event was the marriage of Charles Kenyon, a soldier from Ft. McDowell, and Sarah Moore, the daughter of a freighter, in 1872. The wedding was celebrated in conjunction with the grand opening of the Goldwater store: "all the swell society of the town [attended] and the officers from McDowell who chanced to be here participated. The ballroom was an adobe house with a dirt floor, and when the music started and the young people entered, the doors were closed and nobody was allowed to go home until daylight." Apparently, Phoenix pioneers did indeed party all night until sunrise.

An early reminiscence (1871) by Elizabeth Kirkland Steele provides more detail of such dances. She described the setting with candlestick holders nailed up all around the room to provide light. Dusty dirt floors were intermittently sprinkled with water. At midnight, a supper was held with pork sausage, spare ribs, sweet potatoes, cake, dried apple pie, hot biscuits, Southern corn pone, bread and black coffee. The revelers danced "til broad daylight," doing the Arkansas Traveler as well as clog dances.

A similar gathering was recounted in 1872. "On Saturday evening, by way of housewarming the youth and beauty of Phoenix and vicinity had a ball in the new house of Mowry and Cotton. At the upper end of the dancing floor, on a raised platform, sat the musicians, a young girl with a harp, a boy with a violin, and a little old man, the father of the other two musicians blowing upon a flute. Between thirty and forty ladies were in attendance and gentlemen in abundance. Dancing was kept up until way in the night which, with flirtation, chit-chat, etc., made the hours pass away pleasantly. After the dance the party repaired to the Capitol House for supper." Similarly, in 1880, Pedro Perez married Anita Ortega on the Balsz ranch, with a "Mexican Orquestra, lots of food ... and plenty of dance till the early hour of the following day."

Quite naturally, there were balls on major event days, such as New Year's Eve. As fraternal organizations (from Masonic Lodges to the

Odd Fellows and Rebekkahs to the Improved Order of the Redman) were developed, annual balls were major social events in the latter part of the decade. A May Day Ball was held "for young people" in 1878. By 1880, there was even a Phoenix Brass Band to "give some entertainment to our young men which will keep them form idleness or worse," as well as The Phoenix Turnvereins. Concerts were often held on the Plaza bandstand, completed in April of 1880. George Loring wrote that the post at Ft. McDowell had a good band.

In 1878, a ball was held, billed as the Washington Birthday Hop, at the Courthouse, with the orchestra under the direction of Professor McNulty. An "elegant supper" was held at midnight. The dance was over by 2:00 a. m., "thus enabling the guests to retire at a reasonable hour." The Redmans Ball was held in March of 1880, and "all of Phoenix Society" was reportedly there. Perhaps not all. The listing of attendees included only one Mexican couple, the Gallardos. The IORM was holding monthly "hops" at Woolsey Hall. The first official observance of the 4th of July was held in Phoenix in 1880, with a barbecue at Buck's Grove, with ice cream and lemonade, and of course, political speeches. Fireworks were later held on the Plaza.

Similarly, festivals were an important part of Mexican social life, events often attended by Anglos. Such festivals included the celebration of San Juan's Day in June, Dia de los Muertas in early November to honor the dead, and the Feast of our Lady of Guadaloupe in early December. In September of 1879, there was a celebration of Mexican independence, observed with fireworks and dancing.

Both Mexican and Anglos enjoyed Sunday horse races down Washington Street, before and after the Sabre Slasher incident. By 1878, George Roberts' ranch included a private race track and a prize purse of $130. Ves Brooks from Yavapai County won both races that June. In December, Hi McDonald won $150 for the 600 yard horse race.

Young children and possibly even adults gathered to watch the freight teams coming into town. Mabel Hancock recalled that "Children learned to look to the west to sight the fascinating cloud of yellow dust rising in the air. The advent of the arrival from the world beyond the desert always stirred the town ... By the time the oxen were near enough to bring the squeak of the wheels to the ears of the children, they could count the two canvas top heavy wagons rolling slowly towards the very spot where they stood." And, of course, the circus was for everyone. There are newspaper references in the late 1870s to Ned Tracy's circus, Jones' Variety Shows, and Ryland's Circus Troupe (in the 1880 Census, the Ryland family is listed as living in Phoenix that summer). In 1878, the *Salt River Herald* reported that Ryland's "Great American Circus" was in town, with bareback riding, rope walking, animals, tumbling and comical acts. "India rubber boy tied himself up in a knot and then unraveled himself." In 1879 Jones' Variety Troupe advertised that its acts were "strictly moral and entertaining." Admission price was one dollar.

George Loring wrote an amusing description of his first circus in Phoenix in 1876. George watched as a "little Mexican band" led the circus into town. "it was enough to make one weep to hear it ... Next came a six mule team with a small bear tied to the back end ... The manager was dressed to resemble a clown and rode a mule ... Where three or four men where standing he would ride from one side of the street to the other, and hand them one of those glaring circus bills, (I have enclosed one of course you have seen circus bills and will not be surprised or believe half of the wonderful performances advertised) ... Then came four more greasers [George apparently had quickly appropriated the negative Anglo term of contempt for Mexicans] ... With a bird cage ... The next two where the last I took them to be the great English Bro's, one was a white man and the other was a greaser ... Dressed in half Spanish and half circus costume ... At night when the mammoth band struck up I thought I would take a walk up to the circus ground [likely at or near the Plaza]. The band men where blowing away as if they where trying their best to bust their horns. In a long row set Mexicans in the dirt the great manager was scoched likewise, viewing his great band and enormous stretch of canvas. the tent had no top nor any seats on the inside. They have so very little excitement here, that quite a number turned out." The story was anticlimactic for during the first act, rains came down, tickets were refunded, and a show was slated for the next night.

In addition to the circus, other performers came to town in the late 1870s. The Taylor Comedy Company arrived in March of 1879, featuring Mattie, "the Queen of Comedy and Song." In December of 1880, the Nellie Boyd Troupe came to Phoenix for a week to perform at Woolsey Hall, following shows in Tombstone and Tucson. This was the first time that an established performer from the East had ventured into the Arizona Territory. The *Arizona Weekly Star* in Tucson wrote, "The arrival of a dramatic company ... marks a new era in our advancing civilization."

The range of presentations was quite impressive. "Fanchon the Cricket", an 1862 play, was about a mysterious young country girl, raised by her grandmother, a reputed witch. The play's tension revolved around the love that developed with the son of a well-to-do upper class family. The signature of the play was the famous "Shadow Dance." "Two Orphans" was an 1874 translation of a French play about the harrowing experience of two sisters separated in Paris. "East Lynne", from 1863, was the adaptation of a popular Victorian novel involving infidelity, a double-identity, and forgiveness. "A Celebrated Case" was a play by the same French author of "Two Orphans." It was a story about a soldier in the French Army, falsely imprisoned for the murder of his wife. The performances in this small frontier town were well-attended, as reported by *The Phoenix Herald.*

While it is not clear if there was a drama club, as existed in Prescott, in 1878 it was reported that two plays were held at the Phoenix Union Sunday School, likely held in the adobe public school, where "Seeing the Elephant" was performed. This was perhaps the popular burlesque of mining life in California gold rush days or possibly the story of the tribulations encountered along the several emigrant trails west. The phrase was often used in conjunction with pioneer descriptions of arduous conditions or situations. Dr. Wharton played the lead character, while other actors included Flora Murray, Bill Breckenridge, and Matt Larkin, playing in "Irish character." There was also a report of a local minstrel group, the "Phoenix Agreeables."

In addition to horse racing, the *Salt River Herald* reported in 1878 that "croquet is now all the fashion," with grounds adjoining the Phoenix Pavilion, perhaps on the Plaza. There was a skating rink in Wentworth Hall, with admission and skates for fifty cents. In addition, "Baseball played an important part of life in those days," according to David Goldberg, the merchant's son, who played first base and catcher. The *Salt River Herald* ran a poem on the front page in 1878, "The Baseball Player" -

The boy stood squarely on the base
Already two were out
The grin that lighted up his face
Shone round about his snout.

The boy, he raised the ash aloft
And called for one hip-high,
The pitcher put it in redhot,
It hit him in the eye.

Again the gallant youth stood up
Determined he would score.
The next one hit him in the stomach,
He playeth ball no more.

It was not until the winter of 1879-1880 (one year after David Goldberg arrived in Phoenix from California, to join with his brother, Aaron, in the store) that baseball is reported in the *Phoenix Herald.* A front page story proudly announced that the Phoenix Club beat the Chaffee Club from Fort McDowell, 13-9, and "was one of the best games ever played in the Territory." Goldberg was joined by Helmich (pitcher) and Kirkland, Lount, Wharton, Stroud, McNulty and others. Another game between the two teams in January, 1880 went into an extra inning, and was won again by Phoenix, by a score of 32-29. There were 75 hits between the two teams.

Later that month, the Chaffee Club blasted Phoenix, 54-17. The game was played on the post grounds, with a ball and supper afterwards. When the game later returned to Phoenix, a ball was also held, at Wentworth Hall.

In March of 1880, it was reported that the "Young Americas" would play the "Mesa boys." Phoenix won, 45-32. Sheets and Wharton were the prominent names. While reporting on baseball largely disappeared from the paper in 1880, it was reported that Goldberg had re-organized the Phoenix baseball club and late in the year hosted the Ft. McDowell team, putting them up at the Bank Exchange Hotel.

By 1880, town life certainly offered a varied social life. But that was not necessarily true for all of its inhabitants. Many must surely have lived in poverty. The *Salt River Herald* reported in 1878 that "The Mexican serves unskilled labor in Arizona in the same manner that the Chinese do in California," working for $1 dollar to $1.50 per day. The public response to poverty, the indigent and sick in frontier Phoenix was weak and intermittent. The first mention of these problems appeared in the minutes of the County Board of Supervisors in 1874 in the midst of difficult financial times in the Salt River Valley and across the nation. There was a reference to a payment to J. J. Gardiner for "board of pauper." In 1875, the Board moved to accept proposals "for taking care of the Paupers of said County" but no proposals, if received, were ever acted upon. In 1876, there were several payments to individuals for boarding of paupers and one payment of $43.75 to A. Goldman for furnishing clothing to the indigent. By 1877, apparently concerned with increased costs, the Board required that all applications for medical assistance must be made directly to the Board for prior approval.

1879 was clearly a difficult year for some, if not many, Phoenix residents. Even the Board of Supervisors referred to it as a "season of unusual depression." The County created an Indigent Sick Fund. A Poor House Fund was also established under John Alsap's management. J. B. Dennis must have rented an adobe dwelling to the County for said purpose, for he was paid $20 to $30 a month in rent. An Emma Stowe was employed as Matron, paid $30 a month plus fifty cents per day for her own board and that of each resident pauper. Dr. Rosson attended to the sick at the Poor House in 1880.

That same year witnessed several insanity cases reviewed by the Board. The first such case occurred in December of 1879, when William Wilson (age 55) was paid $430 to take his wife, Susan (age 25) to the Langdon and Clark Asylum in Stockton, California. (Susan was listed at home in the 1880 Census; in fact, she was likely pregnant at the time of her purported "insanity," for in the Census she and William had recently given birth to a new child.) One Poor House inmate, Alexander Lackwood, was sent to the asylum in California. Christopher Fitzgerald, who had been in jail, was also sent there; a G. W. Brown was paid $200 to transport him. A "Chinaman" was ordered there in October of that year. These were new problems for the frontier town. The farming hamlet was becoming more complex.

Town life in frontier Phoenix was different and more varied in 1881 than in 1870. There was clearly more leisure time for some citizens, allowing for more organized social, cultural and sporting pursuits. "Civilizing" activities like orchestra or band, drama and theater, the library and Literary Association arose with population growth and new perspectives on culture from some of the recent arrivals to Phoenix society. The range of entertainment for a town of 1,700 is perhaps surprising but Phoenix was no longer a remote outpost along the Salt River. It was a city committed to growth and its own definition of a civilized polity.

CHAPTER EIGHT
Gunfights and Lynchings

It was high noon. The sun was blistering hot this summer day in Phoenix. The two gunslingers sauntered warily towards each other down Washington Street. Women, children and shopkeepers hurried in to the protection of their adobe buildings, peering out onto the dusty street with nervous excitement. As the two gunmen drew nearer, their nerves were taut. Who would draw first? An eye twitched, a trigger finger moved and guns started blazing. When the smoke cleared ...

That is the mythical, Hollywood version of good and evil played out in the streets of many a rough and tumble Western town. It is a portrait of town life, far removed from the reality of the previous sketches of pioneer life in Phoenix. Yet violence was indeed a part of frontier town life; it just rarely resulted in that style of gunfight. But with a generally single, male population in the early Arizona Territory, law and order was a primary concern of early settlers. Saloons, the social center for cowboys as well as ranchers, lawyers, merchants and farmers, was an accepted part of town life. Drinking may have relieved the tedium of daily life, substituted for the lack of available women, or served as an escape at times from the summer heat. But such an environment could also lead to arguments and violence. Perhaps the quick resort to violence that resulted in gunplay was simply the residue of the horrific drama many personally experienced in the Civil War. Or in Arizona, perhaps it was an outgrowth of recent violent Indian campaigns that were a part of Territorial history throughout the 1860s and most of the 1870s. No matter how history treats that Anglo-Indian story, the harsh reality for many a Territorial pioneer was the lingering threat of Indian attack on forts, ranches, towns, deserted roads, and stage coaches and the recent memories of such violence.

The fledgling agricultural town of Phoenix was not immune to violence in the 1870s. These incidents had diverse origins. Prominent and respectable citizens resorted to the gun on occasion, not just the stereotypical desperado. The Mexican community, representing nearly half of the population, would have its share of violence. Difficult economic times of the mid-1870s was likely an influence on the increase in crime. It was perceived that improved law and order would provide increased safety for Town residents as well as a stable environment more conducive to growth and prosperity. How justice was meted out in the courtroom and in the streets provides a unique perspective on Phoenix town life and its mores.

Even as Phoenix was being settled by the Swilling Party, disputes arose. One such altercation occurred in August of 1869, when Jim Smith, an original member of the Swilling Party, shot and killed James Nelson. Smith fled and was never brought to justice. A year later, the *Prescott Miner* reported Smith was seen at a ranch near the Hassayampa River, seeking food and water. Shortly after this encounter, it was reported that he was traveling with Indians. That probably did not end well.

At that time, the chief lawman of the Salt River Valley was the Sheriff of Yavapai County. While he may have wanted the votes of the settlers of the Valley, he was not likely to provide much service so far from his home. It was not until February of 1871, when Maricopa County was officially created by the Territory that the new County had its own Sheriff. William Hancock, the Town Surveyor, was appointed by Governor Safford until elections were held later in May.

County Sheriff in those early days in the Arizona Territory was a demanding and complicated position. The Sheriff had many duties - tax assessor and collector, service to the Courts, managing the jail and overseeing prisoners, transporting prisoners and even the insane, and, of course, maintaining the peace, investigating crimes, apprehending and arresting lawbreakers and even performing executions. They were generally poorly paid, relying on a cumbersome fee schedule that paid them for serving a citation, summoning a jury, making a court appearance and travel reimbursement. Fees might range from 50 cents to two to three dollars. Separate amounts were paid to jailers, watchmen, guards, those providing food and to doctors providing medical care. Fees to Sheriffs for tax collection ranged from 5-10% of the property tax valuation (for example, in 1871, County Sheriff Barnum was ordered to collect $4517.93 in taxes; he would have received approximately 8% of all he collected). Due to this financial role of the Sheriff, they had to post bond to ensure honesty in carrying out their prescribed duties. It is not surprising that the early Sheriffs of Maricopa County were generally men of some prominence and even property.

The requirements to be elected to Sheriff did not necessarily require any credible "lawing" experience. Most candidates in the early 1870s probably knew how to handle a gun but were more inclined to keep the peace without resorting to violence. Generally, elections were a spirited affair, and the office more likely to be a popularity contest.

The first such election in Maricopa County in 1871 fits that description. At that time, the rivalry that existed between the original Swilling settlement and the proposed new Phoenix Townsite had raised the political stakes. Each side offered their own candidate for Sheriff. The campaign was apparently a bitter one. The Swilling faction had nominated Jim Favorite, a farmer; while the Townsite group ran John A. ("Gus") Chenowith. Towards the close of the campaign, Chenowith and Favorite quarreled at the latter's ranch. The story is told that Favorite had circulated a rumor alleging he and Chenowith had agreed the winner of the race would appoint the other as the deputy. Favorite apparently dismissed the rumor but refused to publicly retract it. Chenowith went to Favorite's ranch to discuss the matter. Words turned to anger and Favorite shot at Chenowith with a double-barreled shotgun but missed. Chenowith chased Favorite into his corral whereupon he shot between the posts and killed Favorite. Chenowith quickly departed and Tom Barnum (one of the earliest homesteaders and married to an

Osborn) was chosen to replace Chenowith while John Moore, a former Sheriff of Yavapai County, replaced Favorite. Tom Barnum won the first election for Sheriff, 200 votes to 171 votes for Moore.

This, however, was not the end of the story. While John Chenowith may have left the area for a time, until emotions cooled, he must have returned rather quickly, for in August of 1871 he married one of the several eligible Murray daughters, Mary. There is a notation in the Board of Supervisor Minutes that there was a trial. Not surprisingly, since John did have a friend who witnessed the entire affair, John was acquitted. In November of 1871, John and Mary purchased the Milliken ranch east of town. John was both a freighter and farmer. The Chenowith family later moved to New Mexico where John raised cattle and a family of nine children. The Chenowith/Favorite gunfight was apparently not a shocking, disruptive event to local town life and John went on to lead a long life.

Early Lawmen

Following Hancock's brief tenure (no mention is made of him apprehending Chenowith), the following Sheriffs served the community - Thomas Barnum (1871); Thomas Worden (1871-1872); Thomas Hayes (1872-1874); George Mowry (1875-1878); and Reuben Thomas (1879-1881).

Tom Barnum resigned six months into his position. The Board of Supervisors appointed Thomas Worden. Thomas had come to Phoenix from Wickenburg, where he had been a saloon owner (selling out to renowned pioneer, Abraham Peeples). He came to the Salt River Valley in 1870 to seek his fortune in farming, homesteading land near the Salt River Canal, north of the Phoenix Townsite. (In addition to Barnum and Worden, other early farmer/homesteaders became Sheriff later in the 1880s - Lin Orme, Noah Broadway and John B. Montgomery; Reuben Thomas, George Mowry and even future City Marshal Henry Garfias were not successful in claiming land). Worden's neighbors included prominent community members, J. Direly Rumburg and James A. Young. Worden's major accomplishment was likely the construction of the new jail, built by John Averish for his bid of $1200.

Worden lost the very next election to his deputy, Thomas Hayes; sold his homestead and moved to California. Hayes' life in Phoenix is an enigma with little or no public records. While local Phoenix "precinct" constables turned over a good deal, Hayes was able to keep William Fenter (yet another homesteader) as constable during his tenure. He did not run for re-election.

William Hancock's friend and associate, George Mowry triumphed over Lin Orme in the next election in 1875. Mowery was well-known, respected and well-liked. Given his Post Office duties, that he reportedly carried out with enthusiasm and diligence, George must have known everyone in the community. He had originally been appointed County Treasurer by Governor Safford in 1871 and won the first election for that position. In partnership with James Cotton, they built a new store in 1872 on Washington Street, right next to Murphy and Dennis, even using expensive lumber from Prescott. Their first tenant was, of course, a saloon, the scene of much political discussion. At the same time, he had a short-term hand at farming, purchasing the Kinsey Watson homestead in 1874, only to sell it to Judge Tweed in January of 1875, netting a $175 profit.

In a letter to the *Weekly Arizona Miner*, in November of 1875, a writer observed, "Our town is getting very orderly. Heretofore drunken Indians, making night hideous with their wild orgies, was a continuous nuisance. But that has all stopped, thanks to the decisive actions of our Sheriff George E. Moury (sic) and his deputy, W. D. Fenton (sic)." As noted earlier, Fenter had been serving in that position off and on since 1872. In April of 1877, the Board of Supervisors authorized Sheriff Mowry to procure a suitable house for a "pest house." Dr. Wharton had been appointed Health Officer, due to a purported outbreak of smallpox in the "Mexican quarters." He vaccinated 32 persons but resigned the office within the month, citing a lack of casework. The pest house was not pursued.

In that same year, Sheriff Mowry was consumed with presenting "nuisance" cases to the Court. He cited one lot for having a "filthy" adobe hole; another for washing clothes in a ditch; a Chinese laundry for discharging foul water into a ditch; another Chinese "Butcher" for keeping corrals for cattle and hogs in a "filthy condition." Jesus Otero was cited for allowing manure to accumulate in his corrals to a depth of one to two feet, giving off an "offensive stench," particularly in the summer. The Court ordered that the owners be so notified and be given fifteen days to abate or the Sheriff would do so and charge the costs to the owners.

Mowry's tenure should perhaps best be remembered for instilling a commitment to professional law officers. Hiram McDonald was both a jailer and later Deputy Sheriff, who would serve over 50 years in the Phoenix Police Department. He was also a good example of how lawmen supplemented their income. In 1878, McDonald, Francis Shaw and William Kent discovered gold in the Phoenix Mine, up in the Cave Creek Mining District, 30-odd miles north of Phoenix, that proved to be a valuable strike.

Billy Blankenship was appointed Deputy Sheriff under Mowry and served in that position until 1899, also serving concurrently as City Marshall for six of those years. Thomas Sherman was appointed a Phoenix constable in 1878 and became a Deputy United States Marshall in 1879. Joe Phy, having been a Deputy Sheriff in Pima County, took a similar position in Maricopa County in 1877-78, under Sheriff Mowry. Joe had also worked for Worden earlier in the decade. He actually sought the position of Sheriff of Maricopa County in the 1878 elections, lost and moved back to Tucson. Then, while continuing with both his water and freighting business, he also served as Deputy Sheriff for Pete Gabriel in Florence, Pinal County in the early 1880s. Their initial friendship deteriorated into a bitter feud, leading to the infamous Phy-Gabriel gunfight at the old Tunnel Saloon in Florence on May 31, 1888. Phy was killed with bullets in his stomach, thigh, shoulder and wrist; while Gabriel, albeit severely wounded in the lung, groin and intestines, lived for another ten years.

It was Reuben Thomas that defeated Phy in the 1878 election. Thomas, having arrived in Phoenix as the Superintendent of Wells Fargo, is generally lost to history, despite serving during a very violent time. In June of 1880, there is a record of Sheriff Thomas taking a William Wallace and then a Juan Aria to the Langdon and Clark Pacific Hospital for the insane in Stockton, California for $300 each. Sheriff Thomas' role was likely eclipsed by the two men elected as Phoenix constables in 1878 - Billy Blankenship and Henry Garfias.

(Left to right) Enrique Garfias, Hiram McDonald, Billy Blankenship

Enrique, or Henry Garfias, born in Mexico about 1850, was the first elected Hispanic official in the young Phoenix community. His record and reputation would grow over time. Building upon his service as constable, Garfias ran for City Marshall of the newly-incorporated City of Phoenix, against two Anglos, James Burnett and Thomas Childs. The so-called Citizen's Ticket had nominated Burnett, who had just moved to Phoenix from Prescott a year earlier. Thomas Childs had previously worked as both a constable and jailor. Garfias announced his own candidacy in the papers. *The Herald* opined: "This gentleman in his past official career has given general satisfaction." Both papers educated their readers on the duties of the office. *The Herald* regarded the role of the Marshal as "more of a financial agent than a peace officer." *The Gazette* emphasized the combined duties of "Ex-Officio Assessor, Tax collector, Road Commissioner and Pound-master." Garfias received 97 votes, with Burnett polling 79 and Childs 53, to win the election to a one-year term as the first elected City Marshal. The new $100 monthly salary was still supplemented by several fees: 50 cents for each stray dog killed; three dollars for every conviction in the city recorder's court, and still 8 percent of all taxes collected.

This new position enabled the Garfias family to live a comfortable life. He was the editor of the short-lived Spanish language newspaper, *El Progresso*. In 1884, he was able to purchase lots 2, 4 and 6 in Block 74 and build a home there in 1884-1885. He served eight terms as City Marshal, and was involved in several gunfights into the 1880s, including the Texas cowboy affair. Garfias was also known to have run cattle up at Castle Hot Springs in his later years.

Henry Garfias was living at Jefferson and 3rd Avenue in 1896 when he passed away shortly after a horse accident. *The Gazette* opined that "Arizona has many brave men but for cool determined nerve, coupled with a modest, unassuming manner, Henry Garfias stood at the head." Likewise, *The Phoenix Herald* reported that "for six years, Mr. Garfias was City Marshal of Phoenix and, as such officer, gave the greatest satisfaction to the citizens of Phoenix. He was brave and conscientious and never failed in his duty no matter how much danger menaced him ... [Garfias] had the reputation of never going after a man that did not return with him, dead or alive." It is interesting to note that none of the three English-language newspapers remarked upon Henry being Mexican.

THE LYNCHING DECADE

Despite the existence of a Sheriff's office, a court system and an increasingly responsible group of law officers, the 1870s witnessed a continued resort to vigilantism and lynching, in both Arizona and New Mexico Territories. In the 1870s, public records document 28 lynchings in Arizona and 36 in New Mexico. This actually increased in the 1880s to 63 in New Mexico (60 of those occurring in the period 1880-1884) and 33 in Arizona (26 between 1880-1884). Another 39 legal hangings over that twenty year period occurred in both Territories. Historians generally concede that many lynchings went unrecorded.

In the frontier town of Phoenix, there were five documented lynchings - Ramon Cordova (1872); Mariano Tisnado (1873); George Young (1875); and in 1879, William McCloskey and John Keller. At that same time in 1879, there was the celebrated case of the Mexican Sabre Slasher and in 1880, the first legal hanging in the streets of Phoenix of Demetrio Dominquez. These are their stories.

Ramon Cordova

Stage stations, often located in isolated areas of the Territory, were easy targets for highwaymen and bandits, well into the 1890s. John Baker ran the Blue Water Station on the old Gila Trail in Pima County, 14 miles northwest of Picacho Pass. On the night of December 21, 1871, John Baker, his wife and child were all murdered. The killers were Mexican bandits who would flee back into Sonora, under protection of the Mexican government.

At this time, King Woolsey was running the Stanwix Station at his Agua Caliente Ranch, on the Gila River, 80 miles above Yuma. In early May of 1872, Ramon Cordova was seen working at Stanwix and was recognized by a Judge Anderson, who had purportedly seen him the previous fall in the vicinity of Baker's Blue Water Station. Reporting this to Phoenix authorities, Sheriff Worden and his deputy, Joseph Phy, rode out to the Woolsey ranch and arrested Cordova (another story suggests that Woolsey captured him and held him until Worden and Phy arrived), placing him in the Phoenix jail on May 19, 1872.

The treachery of the "Blue Water Massacre" surely agitated local citizenry. Apparently not trusting the relatively new court system in Maricopa County, vigilantes broke into the jail (jails of the time were notoriously flimsy; this one was located in the rear of the Courthouse in the Hancock/Monihon building on south Washington Street) and hung Ramon Cordova in the cell on the evening of May 21. This was Phoenix's first lynching. Recent border problems with Mexican banditry from 1870-1874 had the *Miner* speculating in late 1871 on the possibility of vigilante action: "The alarming frequency of deeds of violence in our community, and the tardiness with which justice is carried out, will, we fear ... culminate in a vigilance committee, a self-constituted arbiter of justice so common to the frontier where laws are not promptly and strictly enforced." These words proved prophetic.

Similar to other vigilante committees in other frontier towns, no charges were brought against the assailants. Quite often, the sporadic formation of vigilante action was led by Town leaders. Sheriff Worden's whereabouts were not reported. And he was unlikely to arrest his neighbors. The Sheriff did not win the upcoming election and left town shortly thereafter.

Mariano Tisnado

July 2, 1873. Farmer Benjamin Patterson woke that morning to find his cow that he had tethered to a post the night before was now missing. He was able to track the cow and its rustler's horse into the Phoenix Townsite and to the butcher shop of Refugio Subiate. There, the cow's head and hide were found. Upon questioning, Subiate implicated Mariano Tisnado.

Tisnado had been linked to the murder of rancher Benjamin Griffin earlier that same year. He apparently had Griffin's ring on his possession. But no direct evidence had connected him to the crime and he was never charged.

At a brief hearing before the Justice of the Peace, Tisnado admitted to stealing the Patterson cow. On this warm July day, the Courthouse was unusually packed with onlookers for such a nominal offense. Perhaps the citizenry remembered the two murder cases of Manuel Pacheco and Joseph Gentemann, heard by the District Court two months back. In the case of Pacheco, the prosecution witnesses included Sheriff Hayes and other prominent community members such as William

Hancock, James Murray, James Monihon and even John Chenowith. Pedro Sotelo of Phoenix and Manuela Sotelo of Tempe testified on behalf of Pacheco. The jury found Pacheco guilty of first-degree murder, while Gentemann was found not guilty. In a surprising (and unexplained in scant Court records) twist, the verdict against Pacheco was set aside and the case discharged for insufficient evidence.

Tisnado remained in custody to appear before the District Court. That evening of July 2, a crowd of citizens were milling around in the streets of Phoenix. Sheriff Hayes, actually fearing a lynching, slept in the County jail that night. On the morning of July 3, a vigilante group entered the Courthouse, strode across its floors to the jail, and seized Tisnado. Again, the story does not describe Sheriff Hayes' role or whereabouts at this juncture.

The crowd took their prisoner down the street to Monihon's Corral at 1st Avenue between Washington and Adams Streets. As the *Miner* reported, he was strung upon the cross beam of the corral gates, "hanging by the neck ... perfectly dead, with the shackles still on his feet." The crowd quickly dispersed. Again, no charges were brought against the perpetrators and even historian James Barney, writing in the 1950s, would opine: "Such punitive measures, while drastic, were necessary in those early days for the preservation of law and order and the safety of life and property." This type of rationalization also echoed across the frontier of the Arizona Territory.

A similar event occurred three months earlier in Tucson, again reflecting the attitudes of the time regarding lynching in the Territory. Three Mexicans had been jailed for murdering a well-known Mexican couple; another Anglo was being held on an unrelated murder charge. All four were taken from their cells and hung outside the jail in the courthouse plaza. The words of the subsequent jury are illustrative of the tenor of the times: " ... and we further find that said hanging was committed by the people of Tucson en masse; and we do further say that in view of the terrible and bloody murders ... and the tardiness with which justice was meted out ... the extreme measures taken by our fellow citizens this morning, in vindication of their lives, their property, and the peace and good order of society, while it is to be regretted and deplored that such extreme measures were necessary, seem to have been the inevitable results of allowing criminals to escape the penalties of their crimes."

George Young

New Year's Eve, 1875 - the traditional grand ball that year in Phoenix was to be held in the offices of James Grant's stage company. The adobe building had a board floor, conducive for a social gathering and dance. It was a community-wide event.

Lew Bailey, serving as the "floor manager" for the evening, had noticed a recently discharged soldier from Fort McDowell, George Young, stumbling across the dance floor. Lew caught him by the collar and sat him down near the entrance on some sacks of barley to sober up. Young was not happy and Bailey was compelled to toss him out.

Bailey soon was dancing with Mary Kellogg, one of the eligible young ladies in town. At the end of one of the dances, Lew escorted Mary to the window where the ollas (earthen jars used by Indians and settlers, alike, to store water) hung for refreshment. He served Mary and then filled his own gourd, tipping his head back to drink. Both barrels of a shotgun rang out, striking Bailey in the forehead. He fell to the floor, whereupon Mary quickly placed his bleeding head on her lap, trying to stop the profuse flow of blood with her handkerchief. It was one o'clock in the morning of the New Year.

Thinking Bailey to be mortally wounded, a number of men scoured the town for George Young, to no avail. With the exception of about a dozen men, the rest returned to Grant's stage office and the ball. Lew was watched over by several ladies throughout that morning. The shots had apparently glanced off his forehead while tipping the gourd and his head back for that drink of water.

Later that day of January 1, 1876, it was reported that the body of George Young was found hanging to a cottonwood tree on the John T. Dennis ranch, just northeast of the Phoenix Townsite. No charges were filed. Young was quietly buried at public expense. "And Bailey, to the day of his death [years later], had a very noticeable depression on the front of his head as a constant reminder of his narrow escape from death." Adding insult to injury, he also lost the girl, for Mary Kellogg married Eugene Estabrook in 1878.

The Summer Lynchings of 1879

By 1879, Phoenix was a bustling town of perhaps 1,700 people. "Now Phoenix is being considered by many of the best and most liberal minded businessmen of the territory as the coming town or city of our young commonwealth. The time is not far distant when Phoenix will be without doubt the leading commercial, educational and political center in the territory," proclaimed the *Phoenix Daily Herald.* Town pride and boosterism were alive and well. A month later, in May of 1879, the *Herald* trumpeted, "Phoenix is the quietest and most orderly town in the territory, owing, of course, to her excellent officers." With building construction at a steady pace and the impending arrival of the railroad to nearby Maricopa Wells, such optimism was likely deserved.

But there was cause for citizen concern. There had been a noticeable influx of unemployed workers from the recent halt of railroad construction. In fact, in March of 1879, Sheriff Hayes had been compelled to post the following warning: "NOTICE All idle persons not having any visible means of maintaining themselves, and who live without employment, are notified that they must leave town or they will be arrested as vagrants and dealt with according to the law."

While incomplete Justice Court records do not permit long-term comparisons, it is clear that by 1878, Phoenix was experiencing some level of social disorder. In 1878, there were 39 "drunk and disorderly" cases, committed by 19 Mexicans, 16 Anglos and 4 Indians. From January

1, 1879 through August of that year, there were 25 such incidents. Several of these occurred directly in front of five different saloons. One of the 25 was a woman convicted of "disorderly conduct and disturbing the peace and quiet of the neighborhood." Larceny and assault cases were on the rise.

These 1879 cases resulted in different resolutions. Several drunk and disorderly cases, being first offenses, were simply dismissed. Mary Hennessey was fined the typical $10. Several offenders chose to serve jail terms, ranging from 3 to 10 days; most being in the 5-day range. In comparison, an assault and battery conviction led to no jail time but a $35 fine. Another similar case resulted in just a $15 fine. A larceny conviction brought 15 days in jail. William Davis, who had several drunk and disorderly convictions, and defaulted on his fines, was serving 30 days in jail. A. Rapp was found guilty of a drunk and disorderly charge in August of 1879 but the Court discharged him and required that "he leave town to work immediately." The *Territorial Expositor* complained that "Ten dollars fine for a drunken row looks to a man up a tree just a little like fostering and encouraging the business." The same paper was also concerned with light sentencing, arguing that some of the more serious crimes should receive longer sentences, up to the six months provided in the statutes, for "the real use of punishment is to correct men who are drifting into vice."

This was the setting for the explosive events of 1879. The trigger this time was San Juan's Day, a celebration enjoyed by Mexicans and Anglos, alike. It was Sunday afternoon, June 1, 1879 and 200-300 settlers were gathered in town to enjoy the horse racing on Washington Street. Then, a startled crowd saw "a Mexican mounted on a fine animal ... approaching with a drawn saber in his hand. Upon reaching the crowd, he dashed through, striking right and left with his weapon." The papers reported that three people were wounded. A year later, an unverified report suggested one victim had died from wounds received that day.

The assailant, later identified as Jesus Romero, headed east on Washington Street, with shaken townspeople now firing belated shots.

On his way south to Tucson, Romero attacked a Mexican couple, kidnapping the wife. This news reached Phoenix and Constable Garfias, along with Jesus Vasquez, were dispatched to apprehend the "Sabre Slasher." Two days later, Romero was captured near San Xavier del Bac, south of Tucson. By the morning of June 24, Romero was in the County jail in Phoenix.

Later that same day, Justice Bolan sentenced Romero to six months in jail. The prisoner gave various testimony for his motivation - one, he was just having fun and two, he was trying to impress a girl. Another Town rumor suggested he was mad at Anglos for his brother's recent arrest in Tucson for a stage robbery. In Romero's interview with the *Herald*, he actually expressed some fear of a potential lynching. The paper assured its readers that "the officers have taken measures to prevent such proceedings." The paper later reported in July that Romero was "clearing off mesquite from town property." On July 12, it was reported that the Town Association trustees were experimenting with prison labor and that some prisoners were refusing to work. The *Herald* editorialized that it supported withholding food to encourage prisoners to work - "No sweat, no bread."

While Romero was working off his jail time, Phoenix seemed to return to some calm. Then, on August 19, towards the end of another hot summer day, tragedy struck - Luke Monihon had been murdered, shot in the back, on his way home to his farm, three miles southwest of town. He was found 200 yards from his home. While a doctor was summoned, Monihon passed away that evening, without ever regaining consciousness.

The next morning, Henry Garfias, Billy Blankenship and an Indian tracker, were on the hunt. The constables tracked the assailant to the home of A. J. Wilcoxson, Luke Monihon's father-in-law. John Keller was arrested there without conflict and taken to County jail on August 20. While Wilcoxson was arrested as a possible accomplice, he was discharged within a few days. His relationship to the murderer of his own daughter's husband was never explained. Luke Monihon was mourned by the town. His brother was the prosperous and well-liked pioneer, James D. Monihon, who would later serve as Phoenix Mayor in the 1890s.

With Romero's light sentence and now Keller's cowardly and unprovoked deed, the whispers of a possible lynching became more audible. Garfias recalled "that the lives of both Keller and Romero were in danger, and as Keller was my prisoner I demanded of McDonald that he give him up to me ... intending to take him to Fort McDowell. I also asked him to turn over Romero to me for the same purpose. He said he would turn them over to me at dark that evening."

But that was not to be. At 5:00 p. m. on August 21, Jesus Romero (perhaps even hearing in jail of a possible lynching) attempted to escape while being moved to another cell. He was shot several times by Hi McDonald and attorney, J. W. Stephenson. The bullets caused Romero to reel away in a circle, but he again came at them with a large piece of redwood plank, raised to strike. McDonald fired another shot and the prisoner fell dead. The coroner's jury would later rule that it was justifiable homicide.

The evening's events to come would only increase the community's desire for retribution. About midnight, Johnny LeBarr closed the doors of his Palace Saloon and crossed Washington Street to share some drinks at the saloon of Brown and Daniels. He would regret not simply going to the rear of his own saloon and house to his wife and children. While drinking with some of his friends, LeBarr apparently refused to drink with one, William McCloskey. (One pioneer story suggested LeBarr was trying to arouse a mob to lynch Keller and McCloskey refused to join.) McCloskey, angered by the rejection, attempted to pick a fight with LeBarr, to no avail. McCloskey left but returned in minutes and plunged a knife into the abdomen of a surprised LeBarr. McCloskey was captured two blocks away. LeBarr was carried to his home where he died at 6:00 a. m. on the 22nd.

By 10:00 a.m. that same morning, Marion Slankard, a farmer by trade but who had been designated "Captain" by his fellow townsmen, led the "Law and Order Committee" to the County courthouse and jail. Sheriff Thomas and Constables Garfias and Blankenship were nowhere to be found (it is not clear why Garfias did not transport Keller from the jail that previous evening). Hi McDonald had the unenviable task of being left in charge of the jail by himself. With guns drawn, the Committee demanded that McDonald hand over the prisoners. Within moments, Keller and McClosky had ropes tied around their necks as they were led to the town Plaza. In their last words, Keller alluded to an old grudge with Monihon (other rumors suggested Keller, who had worked at Monihon's farm, was infatuated with his wife); while McClosky blamed the incident on being drunk.

Ropes were thrown over a cottonwood tree on the northwest corner of the Plaza. A freight wagon was commandeered and Keller was placed on the wagon. According to an eyewitness, Keller fainted as he was put on the wagon; as the wagon was driven out from under him, he fell off the wagon, with the rope being drawn tighter around his neck. But the thrust did not break his neck as intended; rather, he choked to death in front of the on-lookers. In a similar manner, McCloskey was then placed on the wagon. Seeing what had transpired with Keller, McCloskey actually jumped off the wagon as it moved forward, thereby quickly breaking his neck.

Slankard spoke to the crowd, warning troublemakers to leave and Mexicans to avoid causing a disturbance over the Romero killing. That afternoon, safely back in town, Sheriff Thomas again posted that same notice warning the idle and unemployed to leave town. Judge Porter denounced the affair as a "cowardly murder" but told the Grand Jury that it could choose simply to let the matter rest. The foreman of that jury investigating the lynching, respected pioneer leader Charles T. Hayden, founder of Tempe, had these words: "We find that the revolutionary nature of the action of the men who caused the hanging of two men in the streets of Phoenix on the 22nd day of August last was aided and abetted by so large a number of our best citizens, that we have to admit with shame that the Grand Jury and Court cannot execute our laws, and ask to be discharged."

The *Herald* probably spoke for the community: "While we deprecate mob law ... under the circumstances we cannot say aught against it ... No violence or rowdyism was allowed and the best order prevailed." Their headline was telling - "A Bloody Week in Phoenix Ends with a Grand Neck-tie Party." The *Expositor* wrote that "the whole was done so quietly."

A week later, the *Herald* noted that "a large number of loungers" have departed after the hangings. And another week later opined that "too much leniency has, we think, been extended to the criminals in the Territory ... [these hangings] should warn other natural born devils to think before they act." A year later, recounting the lynchings, the *Herald* opined that "Prompt and decisive action was needed. The town was filled with rough characters, and this bloody work, once started, there would be no telling where it would end."

The rival *Expositor* surprisingly weighed in against the lynchings in the summer of 1879. In an article entitled, "Judge Lynch Supreme," the editor wrote - "We never approve these acts of violence and cannot now, for there is no reason given by the advocates of lynch law that convinces our mind, and we fear that all such acts give to the opponents of human liberty their greatest arguments against popular government." In another article, an alarm was sounded about the price of progress. "Four stage robberies within three months; seven homicides within a week ... two of the homicides were not of the regular order. They were the work of the Law and Order Committee and we are told that these later homicides were not only deserved, but were good, useful and necessary ... Where did the Law and Order Committee get their warrants? ... Would not the same evidence that satisfied the Committee be equally convincing to a Jury?"

Demetrio Dominguez

It was not evident that either the lynchings or the newspaper editorials had returned Phoenix to some sense of normalcy. In January of 1880, the *Expositor* reported on the killing of Juan Abrigo. The story was recounted that Abrigo had recently thrown his woman (probably common-law wife) out of the house and she had sought refuge with Constable Garfias' wife, Elena. Upon hearing this, Abrigo went over to the Garfias home and literally pulled his wife out of the adobe by her hair. Constable Garfias secured a warrant and found Abrigo working at the new school house doing some carpentry work. Garfias ordered him to "Throw up your hands." Abrigo fired upon the constable, whereupon Garfias shot him dead.

In May of 1880, Sheriff Thomas was still publicly warning vagrants that they could be arrested. Court records in 1880 indicate that cases involving drunk and disorderly, disturbing the peace, and indecent exposure incidents were down somewhat from 1879 and certainly from those of 1878. Total offenses amounted to only 23 over the 12-month period, committed by 15 Anglos, 7 Mexicans and 1 Indian. Eight of the cases had their charges dismissed "on the promise of good behavior." One of them was advised "to go from town ... and behave yourself in the future." There were several assault cases and a handful of larceny crimes during this period. One noted new situation was the emergence of violent crime by the recently-arrived Chinese, assaults and murder of other Chinese, totalling four in late 1879 through 1880. Perhaps this also reflected a willingness to take their cases to an American court, as well.

The singular episode of notoriety in 1880 was the first legal hanging in Phoenix. The guilty party was Demetrio Dominguez. He and two other bandits had robbed the Prescott to Phoenix stage along Black Canyon, within two miles of the Gillette station. Two men on the stage were killed, one of them unarmed yet savagely attacked by gunfire and knife stabs. It is not known exactly when nor how Dominguez was apprehended, nor how the other two managed to evade justice.

Dominguez was found guilty by jury one year later in October of 1880 and sentenced to hang on November 26. Sheriff Thomas had the gallows constructed a half-mile from the jail, conveniently next to the cemetery, necessitating a long walk through a hostile crowd. The Sheriff employed a contingent of fifteen men to escort Dominquez to the gallows. The next day the *Herald's* headline read: "HUNG Demetrio Dominguez Dangles Downward."

It is tempting to characterize frontier Phoenix and its mores on law and order by simply focusing on infamous lynchings and hangings. Certainly, the murders and the town's response through the 1870s suggest a ready willingness on the part of the criminal as well as the town's citizenry to resort to violence. The local press throughout the Territory contributed to this sense of helplessness with its portrayal of an inadequate legal process. Even though citizens elected the Sheriff, the constables and the judges, the propensity to safeguard the community through extra-legal means was an ever-present course of action, requiring just the right stimulus and circumstance. As towns in the Territory began to grow and prosper and the Indian conflict subsided, the need to protect and preserve life and property by any means necessary began to subside by the mid-1880s.

CRIMES AND OTHER MISDEMEANORS

It is equally tempting to characterize the criminal as the vagrant and the desperado. The above notorious cases reinforce that Western image. While County court records are sporadic, a closer look reveals that crime was not limited to these highly-publicized events. Nor was it simply the work of "natural born devils." Even prominent individuals of Phoenix were capable of violence.

The first homicide in the new Townsite was the killing of a Cooley (likely David Cooley) by a saloon keeper on Washington Street in the fall of 1871. The case history has not been recorded. 1872 was a tough year on the Phoenix frontier. William Butts shot and killed fellow farmer, Stephen Connell; again, court results are not known. Perfecto Espinosa got a year in jail for grand larceny. Jose Marie Presiado was found guilty of murder but had already fled the County. Johnny Moore struck Lewis Rodgers over the head with his pistol; was later found guilty and paid a fine of $100. Hugh Brown assaulted someone with a "deadly weapon." John Young was indicted with an intent to commit murder against an Indian; the jury found him guilty and the judge set the verdict aside for some unknown reason. In 1872 at the store of Heyman Menassee, Thomas McGoldrick saved the life of Dan Twomey. Twomey and Mike Connell were exchanging angry words when Connell drew his pistol and pointed at Twomey's head. Just as Connell pressed the trigger, McGoldrick knocked his arm upward and Connell was disarmed. All three men were farmers. McGoldrick had been with the original Swilling Party. Just two years later, Twomey was killed near Fort McDowell by Apaches.

Jack Swilling was known to resort to violence on occasion, in part due to a purported addiction as well as his propensity to drink. There is anecdotal evidence from his contemporaries that one had to be wary of Swilling if he was on a drinking binge. He is reported to have shot a Mexican in 1871 over the loss of the Town elections. In May of 1872, John W. Swilling was indicted for assault with the intent to commit murder. The *Arizona Miner* reported at the same time that "J. W. Swilling cowhided a man for slandering a lady." The name of the victim was not identified. Swilling plead not guilty and the jury agreed with him in their decision in September of that year. In 1878, Swilling would be found guilty, unjustly, of a stagecoach robbery and died in the Yuma jail awaiting justice.

Columbus Gray would suffer no such fate. He lived a long life as one of Phoenix's most revered early settlers. But in 1872, Gray was charged with two separate incidents involving assaults "with a deadly weapon to inflict a bodily injury," one against J. B. Mercer and the other, William Holmes. In the case of the latter trial in September, the prosecution had Joseph Phy and Benjamin Velasco as witnesses, while Gray's witnesses were Benjamen Patterson, A. B. Liles, and Johnny

Moore. He was found not guilty. In the Holmes case, Gray entered a plea of "assault and battery." He was found guilty and ordered to pay a fine of $200 or serve 40 days in jail. Gray paid the fine.

In 1873, there were the aforementioned cases of Pacheco and Gentemann. That same year, Patrick Flynn received seven months in prison for assault with a deadly weapon. A. B. Sorrell, a prominent homesteader/farmer was charged with "exhibiting of a deadly weapon in a rude and angry manner in the presence of two or more persons." Oh Ging, a Chinese settler, received ten years in prison for murder in the second degree.

Throughout the mid-1870s , there are similar levels of serious crime (larceny and assault) and yet, available records suggest that it did not exceed three to five incidents in any year. In 1876 Louis Davis was convicted of assault and was sent to Yuma for 224 days, because he could not pay his $450 fine. In that same year, Louis Bachman embezzled $91 from his employer, Charles Veil, and took some bacon from the store - he was sentenced to two years at the Territorial Prison. In 1879 Ah Sam served 25 days in jail for stealing 10 hams from the very same Charles Veil. There was a pronounced increase in larceny reported in 1878 and 1879 and a particular rise in assault cases 1879, totaling approximately ten, beyond those described above in the summer of that year.

Most cases were handled inside the courtroom. But A.C. Baker, an attorney who arrived from San Francisco in 1879, recounted that Judge Warfield, a Justice of the Peace, often held court on an open lot on Washington Street under a big cottonwood tree. When the Judge ordered a recess, everyone went across the street to get a drink. Court life was apparently a social event at times.

The Case of William Hellings

The incident involving William Hellings began in 1872 in Prescott but played out in the courts of Phoenix in 1874. The murder on Whiskey Row in Prescott showed how a man of some prominence and influence

William Hellings

could work the frontier judicial process. Hellings was an early homesteader and respected businessman, opening the successful Salt River Flour Mill in 1871, at the age of 27. He was a true frontier entrepreneur.

Hellings had initially gone into partnership in Phoenix on the flour mill business with his brother, Edward; C. H. Grubb; and long-time friend from Philadelphia, Edward Grover. For reasons unknown, the partnership had dissolved. But certainly not without some acrimony.

While on business in Prescott, Hellings ran into Grover on Montezuma Street on the night of September 19, 1872. Angry words were exchanged over some aspersions Grover had made about William's brother. Hellings shot an unarmed Grover through his right lung. Turning himself into the Sheriff, he spent the night in the Prescott jail. He was released on bond. The 34-year old Grover died on October 1, 1872. His death resulted in a charge of murder against Hellings.

He quickly retained John A. Rush, perhaps the best criminal lawyer in the Territory, as well as Granville Oury, a lawyer by training but also a well-connected politician. It was not until June of 1873 that the facts were presented to a Yavapai County grand jury. They could not reach an indictment, perhaps persuaded by Hellings' assertion that he thought Grover was reaching for a gun. The case was dismissed.

In yet another twist, the case was re-opened in November of 1873 and this time the jury brought an indictment for murder. He was arrested again; this time his bond was posted by his brother, P. W. Smith and Morris Goldwater. Hellings' attorneys immediately requested a change of venue to Maricopa County due to Hellings' "personal enemies" in Yavapai County who were "manufacturing public sentiment and creating prejudice or bias against him, with a view to procuring his conviction." He was likely referring to his most vocal critic, John Marion, the editor of the *Arizona Miner*. The Court agreed and the case was transferred to Maricopa County where a jury of Hellings' peers and neighbors would certainly have more sympathy for Hellings' fate.

The deposition of Dr. Semig, the attending physician at Grover's lingering death, was valuable to the Hellings defense. Dr. Semig stated that Grover would not answer his question as to whether he [Grover] had actually raised his hand. Grover apparently replied, "well, that aint' for me to say. I cannot say nor do I know what I would have done. I made a mistake in Bill Hellings." In April of 1874, the Maricopa County Grand Jury heard testimony. However, the prosecution's main witness, C. H. Grubb, was not in attendance. His earlier deposition had also been silent as to whether Grover had raised his hand. The case ran, not continuously, into May, where on May 30 closing arguments were made. The jury returned with a verdict of "not guilty" within five minutes.

The *Miner* reported that "The spectators applauded the rendition of the verdict ... everyone started to shake hands with the defendant, and the verdict meets the approval of all who have given evidence or who had watched the progress of the trial." The *Miner* further reported that a picnic celebration was then held at the "garden of G. A. Wilson" (an early pioneer whose homestead was near Hellings' ranch and mill). Even those who came to the trial from Prescott attended.

William Hellings continued the mill operation in Phoenix until losing it in an 1876 foreclosure action to his partner, Charles Veil. But Hellings' entrepreneurial spirit led him to mining in the Cave Creek area where he had privately built the first road in 1873, possibly hoping to create a new town in that area. This mining venture in Cave Creek led to initial success in 1876 but then to failure by 1880, whereupon he relocated to mining interests in Globe. Hellings died in California in 1913, where the previous census had listed his occupation as "mining superintendent." As one historian has written, "he had left behind him the legacy of a man - a murderer perhaps - who escaped the gallows but nevertheless left an indelible mark on the early commercial development of the Arizona Territory."

The Case of Henry Morgan

Another well-respected early pioneer was Henry Morgan. In the 1860s, Henry had started a trading post and ferry along the Gila River, not far from Maricopa Wells. In 1872, he opened a store on Washington Street. Despite his success as a merchant, Morgan had his share of problems with the law. In 1876, Morgan was fined $300 for "assault with a deadly weapon." In 1879, he was charged with the murder of a Mexican, Jesus Figaro, on a complaint made by Lin Orme and J. T. Dennis. Pleading self-defense, the case was dismissed.

1880 was a difficult year. In March, he was arrested on a drunk and disorderly charge. Morgan denied being drunk but plead guilty "to speaking loud and in an angry voice." He was fined $10. Tragically, on July 13, 1880, his good friend and partner, Dan Dietrich, was murdered, shot four times in the back by Indians at Morgan's Ferry. Two weeks later, several Pima Indians attacked Morgan, in retaliation for accusing their chief of assisting in the escape of Dietrich's killers. Records indicate another charge was brought against Morgan that same year; he was found not guilty. There was also a pioneer reminiscence that Morgan had entered Salari's Restaurant on Washington Street, drew his revolver and attempted to shoot P. Bolan but bystanders seized his revolver. This was likely the aforementioned 1880 case. He lost his business in that same time period.

Henry Morgan died destitute in 1900 at age 59. From trading post to town merchant, Morgan was a key figure in the long line of traders and freighters in the Arizona Territory. Perhaps living on the edge of the frontier and living through its isolation and its constant dangers resulted in these sporadic episodes of drinking and violence.

Chenowith, Swilling, Gray, Hellings and Morgan represent only a small sample of the violence that played out in the 1870s. But their stories offer a neglected perspective on the stereotypical profile of the criminals of the frontier. This was not the cowboy town of Abilene or Dodge City nor the rough mining town of Tombstone or Bisbee in the Arizona Territory. Nonetheless, violence erupted in the frontier town of Phoenix, a predominant agricultural community, throughout the decade. It was a part of early town life that has been relatively ignored.

CHAPTER NINE
End of an Era

By 1881, the physical vestiges of frontier Phoenix were beginning to disappear. The agricultural village had been transformed into a thriving town. The civilizing influence created by a more educated business elite and the increasing numbers and role of women would soon assert itself. The political leadership of the early pioneer was waning. The demographics of the town were changing. Phoenix was poised at the door of urban progress.

Hiram Hodge had written in Arizona As It Is or The Coming Country, first published in 1877, that "[Phoenix] is pleasantly situated in the valley of the Salt River ... Well laid out, with a fine growth of shade trees along its principal streets, rendering it pleasant, attractive and beautiful." Hodge even downplayed those hot summer months: "the climate in the summer; though quite warm, is not oppressive or debilitating." A story in the *San Francisco Bulletin* in 1878 exclaimed, "The Salt River ... had made this desert blossom as the rose, and in a few years, it will compare favorably with Santa Clara of the Golden State." However, the writer remarked later in the same article, "The greatest drawback is the excessive heat of June, July and August." Commenting on Phoenix in early 1879, the *Phoenix Herald* trumpeted in its headline, "The Most Enterprising and Progressive Town in Arizona."

These journalists were obviously struck by the progress of Phoenix since its founding in December of 1867. The most apparent change was the remarkable population growth that had occurred. In 1870, there was no Phoenix Townsite; those 320 acres of Section 8 contained perhaps one dwelling. By 1880, there were 1,708 residents in the Townsite and 430 buildings. That is astounding growth and in the middle of the desert. A second perspective on those changes is to compare the growth to the 1870 Census, which had identified the area as "Salt River Valley, Phoenix Post Office." That population number, which is generally recorded as Phoenix' starting population, was 240. The corresponding area population in 1880 (that included such prominent Phoenix pioneering families as the Grays, Linvilles, Kelloggs, Ormes, Osborns, Sears, Issacs and Cartwrights) was 2,462. This is not the balance of Maricopa County but simply the adjacent townships surrounding the Phoenix Townsite. Hence, in this comparison, the population increased 1,000 per cent over the decade 1870-1880. No matter the measuring stick, the growth was substantial and noticed across the Territory and into California.

While the growth was apparent, there had also concurrently been a reported exodus, even characterized as a "stampede," in the mid-1870s. The 1880 Census substantiated this transient mobility of the new desert population, a trend that would continue into the 21st century. While enumeration problems exist with assessing changes in the Mexican population, the Anglo mobility pattern is readily discernible. Of the 82 Anglo heads of household in 1870 (including single males), only 25 remained in 1880. Six of these men were single and nineteen were married. Interestingly, of these nineteen, six had been married at the time of the 1870 Census while thirteen were married during the decade, due to the influx of marriageable Anglo women. Those that stayed were represented by some of the more prominent pioneers - Alsap, Barnum, Buck, Dennis, Gardiner, Gray, Hancock, Murphy, Osborn and the Starar brothers. Darrell Duppa had returned to Phoenix by this time as had the Swilling family, albeit Trinidad was now alone with her children.

With this growth and mobility, the composition of the community had also changed. The Mexican population had increased to 699 within the Phoenix Townsite, and amounted to 41% of the population. When compared to the larger surrounding population (that 2,462 number), the percentage of Mexicans had dropped to 33% (or 822). This was largely due to the nominal number of Mexican farmers and laborers in the surrounding townships. Another noticeable change within the community was the recent arrival of the Chinese. By 1880, there were 109 Chinese (as contrasted with Tucson's 159 and Prescott's 90), only two of whom lived outside the Townsite. Of those 107 living in the Townsite, only four were women.

An additional demographic difference in 1880 was the sharp increase of families. By both recollections and the evidence of the 1870 Census, the earlier population was largely comprised of single males, with only 13 families with children. By 1880, the influx of women, the increase in marriages, natural births, and the in-migration of families all contributed to a population that was much more family-oriented. The rise of schools, churches and fraternal organizations later in the decade reflected the social impact of that change. In 1880, there were 226 families with at least one child, headed by a husband and wife; 156 of those were Anglo families, while 70 were Mexican. Another 27 families were headed by women. That is a significant change from the early days of single ranchers, transplanted miners and laborers. Yet, males still outnumbered females by two to one in 1880. Single men were still prevalent - nearly 750 of them, engaged in a variety of occupations but primarily as farm laborers.

This growth had also brought a diversity within the Anglo population. In 1870, there was indeed a greater presence of settlers from southern states but it was balanced by those from northern states and the foreign-born. By 1880, Anglo place of birth had decidedly shifted due to the impact of the new arrivals. The composition looked like an integrated urban center, particularly within the Phoenix Townsite. Southerners represented 20% of the households, with those from northern states representing approximately 35%. Two new trends emerged: a stronger presence of the foreign-born population (not counting Chinese) representing 25%, primarily involved in retail; and the California influence. Newspapers had been commenting in the latter part of the 1870s about the increase in population to Phoenix from western states, and primarily from California. These settlers now exceeded "southern" households. This information is derived by the family data that showed a migration pattern to California and then to Arizona, as depicted by the birthplace of the children. Even Anglo Phoenix was, by 1881, a group with diverse backgrounds and experiences.

Concurrently, the Townsite was beginning to see the melting pot fragment into certain residential concentrations. Henry Garfias lived with his wife in a predominantly Mexican neighborhood. Jesus Otero was living with his family near Miguel Peralta and his family of eight, with Anglos to one side and Mexicans to the other. Miguel Pesquiera and his extended family of eight lived next door to Herrick, the blacksmith and Johnny George, the saloon keeper, on one side and to the other direction, all Mexicans. There are over a dozen concentrations of Mexicans in the 1880 federal Census for Phoenix (concentrations being more than ten Mexicans living in a cluster). One such enclave was near Lount's ice factory on Washington Street, east of 5th Street; one near Charles McNeil's *Arizona Gazette* on west Washington Street. Several town dwellings also contained significant numbers of unrelated Mexicans - 19, 35 and 18 such residents. The latter was located near Michael Wormser's dwelling on east Washington Street near 4th Street.

This physical segregation was also apparent in social circles. The lack of active involvement in politics reflected a certain unspoken division that existed between Mexicans and Anglos. This is further reinforced by marriage records of the period. There were 98 documented marriages in Maricopa County in the 1870s. Twenty of those were between Mexican couples; sixty-five were between Anglo couples; and only thirteen were Anglo/Mexican marriages. The 1880 Census for Phoenix was even more telling. Of the 264 married Anglos in the Phoenix Townsite, only six were Anglo/Mexican households. This was only an increase of three from 1870. The *Arizona Enterprise* reported in 1878 that "Phoenix is markedly an American town ... The Spanish element is fast taking a back seat." Phoenix Anglo settlers at the end of the frontier era would likely have agreed.

Moreover, to read the local newspapers, neither the Mexican, Chinese or Indian were celebrated for their diverse cultures. In 1879, the *Phoenix Herald* editorialized - "It is a disgrace to a civilized community to be compelled to witness nuisances created by our Mexican residents ... They do their washing and cooking on the sidewalks, and all manner of filth is thrown into the ditches ... They have no outhouses ... Some portions of our town surpass that of the Chinese quarters in San Francisco." Similarly, the recently-arrived Chinese quickly gravitated to certain areas of the Townsite.

In one area located near Ah How's laundry and Lung Wing's store, there were three dwellings containing 17 Chinese. In another instance, surrounded by Mexicans, 16 Chinese resided in four dwellings; and in yet another part of the Townsite, 15 Chinese resided in six dwellings, in the midst of Anglo and Mexican settlers.

The Chinese, or "yellow heathen" were urged "to go to New York" in the *Phoenix Herald* in early 1880. The newspaper wanted to see "fewer Chinamen in Phoenix." Townspeople were apparently concerned over opium dens that "are corrupting our youth ... reducing to lunacy our manhood, and degrading our community." The hysteria in California had worked its way to the Arizona Territory. It would finally work its way to the halls of Congress, with the Chinese Exclusion Act of 1882.

As for the Indian in town, the views had changed markedly from 1868 to 1881. A correspondent to the *Arizona Miner* in the earliest days of the Phoenix settlement had this to report - "Since the settlement was started, we have not been troubled by the Apache. We often receive a visit from the Pima and Maricopa Indians, whose friendly relations towards the whites cannot be questioned ... When they are around, one can feel a degree of safety not otherwise felt, as they are ever vigilant." After the Apache wars subsided, this sentiment disappeared. The prevailing attitude viewed the Indian as a "nuisance," with complaints of lounging around on the Plaza, and scantily-clad at that. Mabel Hancock recalled that Indians considered "a gee string adequate clothing" in the summer. Some town ladies placed trousers on a tree outside town for

Indians to wear. This did not prove successful, for one of the first ordinances adopted by the newly-incorporated city in May of 1881 made it illegal for Indians to appear in the city "without sufficient clothing to cover the person," or for an Indian to be "in the city after dark unless employed by a City resident." This was no longer covert discrimination.

The Town's economy had also changed over this frontier era. While still largely based on agriculture (an estimated 15,000 acres under cultivation in the Salt River Valley, with most of that planted in wheat), the retail and service sectors were significant, meeting a broader range of consumer demand, created by that diverse and growing population. Within the Phoenix Townsite, the Arizona Business Directory of 1881, found 98 businesses: 25% in retail, 54% in services and 8% in construction. Small manufacturing represented only four businesses.

The most significant category were the mercantile shops along Washington Street. Mary Gray had recalled the utter lack of consumer goods in 1868. This was not the case in 1881. Goods came from both the east and west coasts. Phoenix freight teams traveled to Yuma and the rail depot at Maricopa to bring goods to the Valley's consumers. Stores offered a wide assortment of general merchandise, as noted in their newspaper advertisements, as well as greater specialization.

The original Phoenix Townsite had, by 1881, become a thriving center of regional commerce. The "adobe" town was beginning to shed its frontier look with the increasing use of brick and even lumber. A correspondent to the *San Francisco Bulletin* wrote at the time that "Phoenix is a busy, thriving town ... an oasis in the desert ... wide streets and cottonwood trees." Mexicans, Chinese and Anglo; rich and poor; merchant and laborer - all lived and worked within this pedestrian and horse and buggy environment. The Monihons lived near two Chinese dwellings. James Cotton and his wife and child lived next to the *Territorial Expositor*. William Hancock's family lived next door to a butcher and a saloon. The Alsaps lived next door to several saloons and a butcher, as well. And the list goes on. The original Phoenix

Townsite had seen much growth and change. As the Townsite developed within its original boundaries, this mixture and diversity was a logical outgrowth. The frontier Phoenix Townsite in 1881 had developed into a diverse collection of uses and cultures. This would be the high point of such an integrated, mixed-use community.

This growth, physical and economic, in agriculture and goods and services, did not go unnoticed. The *Territorial Expositor*, in January of 1880, wrote of its expectation of a large increase in immigration. "Maricopa County offers more inducement to farmers, fruit-growers and industrious people generally." It noted that land was "open for homestead and pre-emption" between Phoenix and Gila Bend that "can be irrigated at reasonable cost ... to the old settlers of this valley we say content yourselves with the possession of 160 acres, for that is as much as any of you can attend to properly, and the family that can well cultivate so much land is rich indeed." With such favorable views towards the economy and its agricultural base, it is no surprise that future progress looked bright. *The Phoenix Herald* postulated at this same time that Phoenix will be "the political, social and educational capital of Arizona."

Thus, on the eve of a new decade, with signs of progress everywhere, the vestige of the frontier era, the Salt River Valley Town Association, no longer appeared to be the best governing organization with which to move the community forward. In August of 1878, the *Phoenix Herald* reported that "Phoenix is now of sufficient size and importance to justify an incorporation. To be sure, it would increase the taxes slightly, but the benefits that would be derived would be worth many times the amount they paid." The same paper, concerned with the condition of ditches once again, carried an editorial in June of 1879 - "It has often been remarked [that incorporation] would improve health and morals ... We have the handsomest village in Arizona ... Let not its bright prospects for the future be blasted by a want of proper care in those things that go to make it a healthful, cheerful place."

What was needed, many had concluded by 1880, was the incorporation of the Phoenix Townsite. Charles Luke, a leading proponent, decried that the current Association commissioners lacked the funds to provide adequate services. Incorporation would make Phoenix government "as economical a one as possible." The petition circulating by December of 1880 had provisions to limit the power of officials to levy property taxes in excess of 0.50 percent of assessed valuation; called for a balanced budget; and required approval of 70% of the voters for Phoenix to issue debt for improvements outside of the annual budget. The petition proposing incorporation, supported by a large number of property owners and businesses, was favorably approved by the Eleventh Territorial Legislature. The Phoenix Charter Bill was signed into law on February 25, 1881, by Governor John C. Fremont.

In May of that year, John Alsap won the first election for Mayor by defeating James Monihon, another early pioneer, by seven votes. Thomas Brown, saloon keeper; John Burger, blacksmith; and property owner, James Cotton were the first Phoenix City Council members. Banker and recent newcomer, Martin Kales was elected Treasurer. Constable Henry Garfias became the first elected City Marshal. This was the height of early pioneer influence on Townsite politics. A new era was emerging, and with the exception of the election of James Monihon to Mayor in the 1890s, new business leadership would arise to steer the progress of the City of Phoenix.

With negligible physical evidence from this era, and no local history museum to celebrate territorial Phoenix and beyond, the frontier period has been largely forgotten in the midst of contemporary, unbridled progress. However, looking back, the legacy of that frontier era was profound.

The vision that created the wide and later, cottonwood tree-lined, Washington Street, predestined its commercial and governmental role, continuing into the 21st century. The two public blocks reserved for government resulted in the Maricopa County Courthouse and a Phoenix City Hall in the 1880s. The adopted grid system for the Townsite became the standard, for good or ill, for future regional development.

Locating the Townsite a distance from the Salt River was likely good planning, given the flooding potential, albeit that decision eventually relegated the river, as in many other cities, to future industrial use.

Homesteading became a predominant form of land purchase throughout the region for decades, even into the 1930s, when it was finally terminated by Executive Order of President Franklin D. Roosevelt. The immediate future expansion of the newly-incorporated City of Phoenix, the platted subdivisions of the early 1880s, were laid out on the 160-acre tracts of a number of prominent homesteaders - Neahr's Addition, Dennis Addition, Murphy Addition and the Capitol Addition.

Early governance, while somewhat reactive and with limited powers, set the foundation for future leadership. Early pioneer settlers responded to the need for public service. Men and women led the movement for public schools, new churches, law and order and support for new roads to connect to commerce. The first City elections reflected that confidence in proven pioneer leaders.

The Anglo culture had begun to assert itself by 1881. While generally not publicly expressed, Phoenix was not Tucson and wanted to shed its adobe appearance and heritage. Mexican festivals continued to bring together both Anglos and Mexicans; yet, the latter group was not represented in community leadership circles. Despite Garfias' multiple elections to City Marshal, Mexicans were not to play an important role in City government until the 21st century, a telling commentary on Phoenix's attitudes towards inclusivity and diversity.

Finally, by 1881, the water resources of the Salt River had largely been captured. The desert, long-described in literature and history as uninhabitable, had been conquered. It was now prime real estate with agriculture practiced on both sides of the Salt River. Canals became the lifeblood of the Valley. Even today, water availability is the key to the growth of Phoenix and the rest of the Salt River Valley. Pioneers would be astonished that discussions and negotiations over water rights are now are held at multi-state levels.

This control of the waterways came with a price. Water usage by new settlers and the construction of later dams exerted a detrimental impact on the once-thriving agricultural land of the Pima, with water from both the Salt River and Gila River being diverted to the new farmers prior to its usual flow into the Indian reservations. The ecological cost has never been truly assessed in light of the apparent progress of civilization. But gone are the cottonwoods and the native Arizona fish and the riverine habitat that would normally occupy the Salt River corridor, albeit efforts are underway to restore sections of the river's landscape. Wandering along those nascent areas today brings to life what trappers and explorers must have witnessed when they encountered the beautiful, lush, riparian habitat of the Salt River.

The story of the frontier West is often depicted in terms of mining discovery, legendary gunfights and lawmen, and military conquest, first of the Spanish and Mexicans, and then of the Indians. These stories of frontier Phoenix depict another side of manifest destiny. The role of settlement was the foundation for the extension of American civilization. The resilience, opportunism, optimism and civic leadership of these early frontier settlers of Phoenix made settlement along the Salt River in the heart of the Sonoran Desert a reality.

APPENDIX
Phoenix Homesteaders
Master List

Phoenix Townsite

Name	Township	Claim Entry Date	Final Patent Date
John Alsap	2N/3E	06/1873	04/1874
Ulysses R. Baker	1N/2E	11/77	09/80
Aaron Barnett	1N/2E	10/70	05/72
Thomas Barnum	1N/3E	06/73	04/74
Charles Bland	1N/2E	02/76	08/76
Noah Broadway	1N/3E	11/71	04/77
Thomas Bryan	1N/2E	12/78	01/86
George Buck	1N/3E	12/70	06/73
James Buck	1N/3E	11/70	06/73
John Burger	1N/2E	01/79	05/83
Jasper Cartwright	2N/2E	08/77	07/81
Reeves Cartwright	2N/2E	09/80	10/84
Dietrich Clasan	1N/2E	01/71	07/73
George Collins	1N/2E	03/76	07/88
John T. Dennis	1N/3E	12/70	08/73
William Downard	1N/2E	09/77	10/83
Brian P.D. Dupper	1N/3E	07/71	07/72
Sarah A. Edgar	1N/3E	03/78	05/85
Michael Engasser	1N/2E	03/78	06/84
Andres Escobar	1N/2E	04/78	11/78
Eugene Estabrook	2N/3E	03/78	08/81
William Fenter	1N/2E	08/75	05/81
Frederick Gatke	1N/2E	06/78	11/85
Jesus Gonzalez	1N/3E	08/79	05/83
Columbus Gray	1N/3E	04/70	10/72
Hosea Greenhaw	1N/3E	12/70	06/75
Martin Griffin	1N/2E	02/76	02/83
Martin Griffin	1N/3E	11/70	06/73
William Hancock	2N/2E	07/78	07/78
Theodore Hanson	1N/3E	02/78	08/85
Eli T. Hargrave	2N/2E	09/78	08/81

Name	Township	Claim Entry Date	Final Patent Date
Eli T. Hargrave	1N/3E	01/71	10/73
William Hellings	1N/3E	09/70	03/72
James Holcomb (2)	2N/3E	12/76	11/81
A.J. Hoskin	2N/3E	12/78	05/89
William B. Howell	2N/2E	05/78	05/81
John Henry Issac	2N/2E	10/78	06/81
William Issac	1N/2E	04/78	06/81
Benjamen Kellogg	1N/3E	12/72	10/76
Owen Kellogg	2N/2E	08/78	08/81
Abraham Liles	1N/3E	03/71	08/73
Antonio Lopez	1N/2E	10/71	11/72
John Lutgerding	1N/2E	01/76	03/82
James D. Miller	1N/2E	07/78	09/80
James P. Moffett	1N/3E	08/78	10/83
James Monihon	1N/2E	07/71	03/78
Luke Monihan	1N/2E	08/75	05/78
Matthew Morrel	1N/2E	08/78	11/79
Niels Morton	1N/2E	12/76	09/78
John Montgomery	1N/3E	03/71	08/72
Almon W. Mowrie	1N/2E	07/78	08/85
James Murphy	1N/3E	12/68	05/73
Peter Nelson	2N/3E	08/71	08/74
Simon Novinger	1N/2E	03/76	08/77
Guadaloupe Ortega	1N/2E	09/71	01/73
John Osborn	1N/3E	03/71	04/74
John Osborn	2N/3E	03/78	05/86
Neri Osborn	2N/3E	07/78	10/81
William Osborn	1N/3E	12/70	04/73
William Osborn	2N/3E	12/78	01/87
Jesus Otero	1N/2E	10/72	11/79
William Parker	1N/2E	08/75	05/85

Name	Township	Claim Entry Date	Final Patent Date
Benjamen Patterson	1N/3E	11/69	06/75
Charles Perkins	2N/3E	08/72	04/73
George Roberts	1N/2E	11/71	03/77
George Roberts	1N/3E	03/78	06/85
Direly Rumburg	1N/3E	10/79	03/82
Direly Rumburg	2N/2E	08/78	05/81
John A. Rush	1N/3E	06/77	12/84
Nicholas Sanches	1N/3E	12/71	07/78
David Schultes	1N/3E	12/70	07/72
Francis Shaw	1N/3E	12/70	09/73
Thomas Shortill	1N/3E	01/71	04/73
Henry Slosser (2)	1N/2E	05/78	02/90
Byran W. Smith	1N/3E	12/70	06/73
Clayton Smith	1N/3E	04/77	10/82
Ahira Sorrells (2)	1N/2E	11/71	02/76
Pedro Sotelo	1N/3E	05/77	04/80
Pedro Sotelo	1N/2E	10/77	08/78
Andrew Starar	1N/3E	01/69	06/73
Jake Starar	1N/3E	07/68	06/73
Andrew Steinaker	1N/3E	01/71	07/73
Emilene Stickney	1N/2E	03/77	11/78
Thomas Taylor	1N/2E	05/77	05/78
Uriah Thompson	1N/2E	09/76	11/77
Lyman Tiffany	1N/2E	10/78	04/82
Daniel Twomey	1N/3E	01/71	01/74
Ludwick Vandemark	1N/3E	04/71	05/72
Charles Veil	1N/3E	09/77	09/80
Patterson Walters	1N/2E	03/77	05/78
James Watkins	2N/2E	09/78	06/91
Kinsey Watson	1N/3E	01/71	09/73
Charles Webster	1N/3E	10/77	02/80

Name	Township	Claim Entry Date	Final Patent Date
John Williams	1N/3E	10/78	06/80
Gordon Wilson	1N/3E	10/68	06/73
Harmon Wilson	1N/2E	05/78	05/81
Thomas Worden	1N/3E	12/70	06/73
Michael Wormser	1N/3E	04/77	04/80
Hans Yaeger	1N/3E	05/77	04/80
James A. Young	1N/3E	03/71	08/72

Note: 93 homesteaders and 103 patents.
A (2) following the homesteader name signifies two patents in the same township.

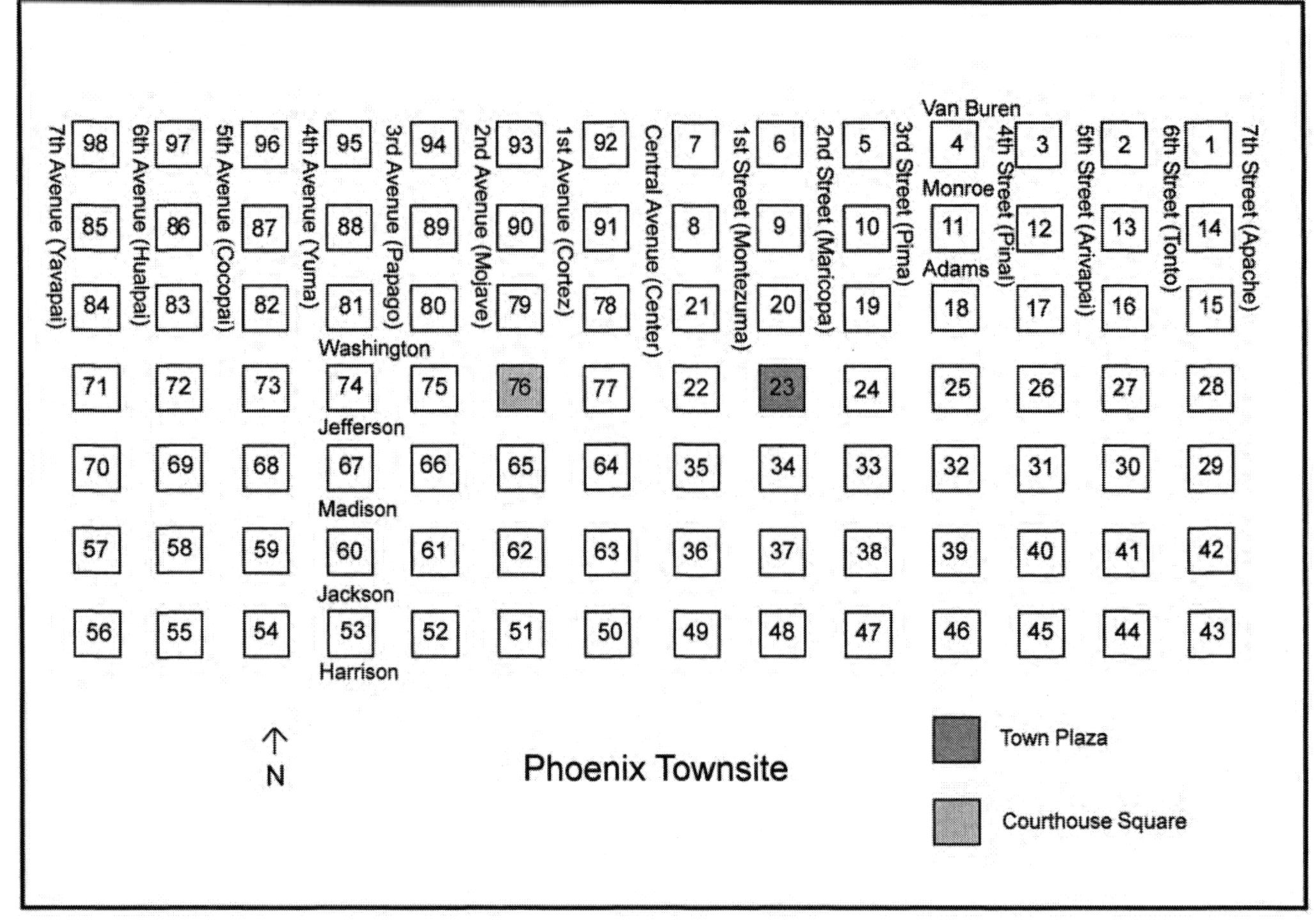
Van Buren
Monroe
Adams
Washington
Jefferson
Madison
Jackson
Harrison
7th Avenue (Yavapai)
6th Avenue (Hualpai)
5th Avenue (Cocopai)
4th Avenue (Yuma)
3rd Avenue (Papago)
2nd Avenue (Mojave)
1st Avenue (Cortez)
Central Avenue (Center)
1st Street (Montezuma)
2nd Street (Maricopa)
3rd Street (Pima)
4th Street (Pinal)
5th Street (Arivapai)
6th Street (Tonto)
7th Street (Apache)
98 97 96 95 94 93 92 7 6 5 4 3 2 1
85 86 87 88 89 90 91 8 9 10 11 12 13 14
84 83 82 81 80 79 78 21 20 19 18 17 16 15
71 72 73 74 75 76 77 22 23 24 25 26 27 28
70 69 68 67 66 65 64 35 34 33 32 31 30 29
57 58 59 60 61 62 63 36 37 38 39 40 41 42
56 55 54 53 52 51 50 49 48 47 46 45 44 43
N
Phoenix Townsite
Town Plaza
Courthouse Square

BIBLIOGRAPHY

Primary Sources

U. S. Census Tabulation, 1830-1930
U. S. National Archives, Individual Land Entry Files
U. S. National Archives, Township Tract Books

Arizona Health Department, Birth and Death Records
Arizona State Library and Archives
    City of Phoenix Tax Assessment Records, 1881/1882
    Maricopa County Tax Assessment Records, 1881
    Minutes of the Board of Maricopa County Commissioners, 1872-1880
    Records of the Justice of the Peace, Maricopa County
    Records of the Superior Court, Maricopa County

Arizona Miner (Prescott)
Salt River Herald; Phoenix Herald
Territorial Expositor (Phoenix)

Phoenix City Directories
Disturnall Directory of Businesses, 1881

John Alsap. "Resources of the Salt River Valley." Paper published in 1872. Reprinted in Arizona Historical Review, July, 1936.
"Interview with A. C. Baker." Arizona Historical Review, October, 1929.
Elmer Cartwright. "Reminiscences." 1940. Arizona Historical Society, Tucson, Arizona

Irene Cartwright Holmes. "A History of the Cartwright Family." 1994. Arizona Collection. Department of Archives and Special Collections. Arizona State University, Tempe, Arizona.

Mantford Cartwright. Letters on Exhibit at the Cave Creek Museum. Cave Creek, Arizona.

Sarah Cartwright Letters, from the personal collection of Linda Cartwright Shank.

J. Goldwater and Brothers, Ehrenburg. Day Book. Morris Goldwater Collection. Arizona Historical Foundation. Tempe, Arizona.

William Hancock Papers. Special Collections, University of Arizona Libraries, Tucson, Arizona.

William Hancock Papers. Small Manuscript Collection. Arizona Historical Foundation, Tempe, Arizona.

Correspondence with Hancock family descendent.

Loring Papers, 1875-1961. Arizona Historical Society. Tucson, Arizona.

Loring Family Letters. Madison R. Loring Collection. Arizona Historical Foundation. Tempe, Arizona.

George H. N. Luhrs. Jr. Oral Interview. June, 1977. Luhrs Papers. Arizona Collection. Department of Archives and Special Collections. Arizona State University. Tempe, Arizona.

James McClintock Papers. Phoenix Public Library. Phoenix, Arizona.

Interview with Osborn family descendent.

Salt River Valley Town Association Minutes, 1875-1876. William A. Hancock Papers. Special Collections. University of Arizona Libraries. Tucson, Arizona.

Salt River Valley Town Association. Small Manuscript Collection. Arizona Historical Foundation. Tempe, Arizona.

Bio Files. Arizona Historical Society. Tucson, Arizona.

Bio Files. Arizona Historical Foundation. Tempe, Arizona.

SECONDARY SOURCES

Aguila, Lourdes, ed. "Farming on the Floodplain." Pueblo Grande Museum, Anthropological Paper No. 11, 2007.

Andrews, John P. and Todd W. Bostwick. Desert Farmers at the River's Edge.Phoenix: Pueblo Grande Museum, 2000.

Ball, Larry. Desert Lawmen: The High Sheriffs of New Mexico and Arizona, 1864-1912. Albuquerque: University of New Mexico Press, 1992.

Barney, James M. "Phoenix - A History of its Pioneer Days and People." Arizona Historical Review, January, 1933.

Barney, James. Articles. Madison Loring Collection. Arizona Historical Foundation, Tempe, Arizona.

Barrios, Frank. Mexicans in Phoenix. Charleston, Chicago, et al: Arcadia Publishing, 2010.

Bates, Albert R. Jack Swilling. Tucson: Wheatmark, 2008.

Bellesiles, Michael. 1877. New York: The New Press, 2010.

Bethard, Wayne. Lotions, Potions and Deadly Elixirs. Lanham, Maryland: Taylor TradePublishing, 2004.

Bostwick, Todd. Beneath the Runways. Phoenix: Pueblo Grande Museum, 2008.

Brown, Dee. The American West. New York: Simon and Schuster, 1994.

Cable, John S. and David E. Doyel. "The Archaeology of Swilling's Ditch: Phoenix's First Historic Canal." City of Phoenix, Aviation Department, 1986.

Carmony, Neil B. and David Brown. Man and Wildlife in Arizona. Phoenix: Arizona Game and Fish Department, 2001.

Carmony, Neil. Whiskey, Six-Guns and Red Light Ladies. Silver City, New Mexico: High-Lonesome Books, 1994.

Cary, Emily. "Crazy Ladies - Women Sent to the Arizona Territorial Asylum for the Insane for Nebulous Reasons." n.d. Web - www.ezinearticles.com.

______. "Pioneering Inmate." 2005. Web - www.chesapeakestyle.com.

Clardy, Susan. Sometimes the Blues. Tucson: Arizona Historical Society, 2007.

Collins, Thomas P. Stage-Struck Settlers in the Sun-Kissed Land. Tucson: Wheatmark,2007.

Czuromi, Carol. "A Short Biography of David Balsz." July, 1969. Balsz School District, Phoenix. Web - www.balsz.k12.az.us.

Dary, David. Entrepreneurs of the Old West. New York: Alfred A. Knopf, 1986.

Dick, Everett. The Lure of the Land. Lincoln, Nebraska: University of Nebraska Press, 1970.

DeJong, David. Stealing the Gila. Tucson: University of Arizona Press, 2009.

Eaton, Jerry. Mesquite to Palms. Phoenix: Central United Methodist Church, 1970.

Elliott, Wallace. History of the Arizona Territory. San Francisco: Wallace W. Elliott and Company, 1884.

Emmons, David. "Theories of Increasing Rainfall and the Timber Culture Act of 1873." Forest History, October, 1971.

Farish, Thomas Edwin. History of Arizona. San Francisco: The Filmer Brothers Electrotype Company, 1915.

Fireman, Floyd S. "The Goldberg Brothers: Arizona Pioneers." American Jewish Archives, April, 1966.

Garcia, Kathleen. Early Phoenix. Charleston, Chicago, et al: Arcadia Publishing, 2008.

Garrison, James. "Adobe Phoenix." Arizona Watch. Arizona State Historic Preservation Office, Fall, 2007.

Goetzmann, William H. Exploration and Empire. Austin: Texas State Historical Association, 2000.

Goldberg, Chet, Jr. "The Goldberg Family of Arizona, 1862-2007." A paper presented to the Phoenix History Museum Ball, April, 2007.

Goldberg, Richard. "Michael Wormser, Capitalist." American Jewish Archives, November, 1973.

Grady, Patrick. Homesteading Along the Creek. Cave Creek, Arizona: Arizona Pioneer Press, 2009.

Greenwald, David H. and Jean H. Ballagh, ed. "The Sky Harbor Project, Early Desert Farming and Irrigation Settlements." SWCA Anthropological Research Paper, Vol. Number Four, 1996

Hamilton, Patrick. The Resources of Arizona. Phoenix: Arizona Territorial Legislature, 1881.

Hanchett, Leland, Jr. Catch the Stage to Phoenix. Phoenix: Pine Rim Publishing, 1998.

Henderson, T. Kathleen, ed. "Hohokam Farming in the Salt River Floodplain." Pueblo Grande Museum, Anthropological Paper No. 9, September, 2003.

Hernandez, Ruben. "A Legacy Lost and Found." Latino Perspectives Media, 2007.

Hinton, Richard. Handbook to Arizona. San Francisco: Payot, Upham and Co., 1878.

Hinz, Judy. How It All Began. Mesa, Arizona: JoAnn Hinz Books, 1989.

Hine, Robert V. and John Mack Faragher. The American West. New Haven and London: Yale University Press, 2000.

Historic Preservation Office, City of Phoenix. "Hispanic Property Survey." September, 2006.

Hodge, Hiram. Arizona As It Was. New York: Hurd and Houghton, 1877.

Howard, Jerry. "Desert Canals: A Hohokam Legacy." Pueblo Grande Museum, Profiles No. 12, 1992.

Johnson, G. Wesley, Jr. Phoenix in the Twentieth Century. Norman: University of Oklahoma Press, 1993.

Judge, Barbara. "Maricopa County Sheriffs." 1987. Small Manuscripts Collection, Arizona Historical Foundation. Tempe, Arizona.

Kaney, Eunice. "Original Phoenix Townsite, Names and Addresses of Citizens and Businesses." Small Manuscript Collection. Arizona Historical Foundation. Tempe, Arizona.

Lamb, Blaine. "Jews in Early Phoenix, 1870-1920." Journal of Arizona History, Autumn, 1977.

Lauer, Charles D. Tales of Arizona Territory. Phoenix: Golden West Publishers, 2008.

Layton, Stanford. To No Privileged Class. Provo, Utah: Brigham Young University, 1988.

Lewis, Christine. "The Early History of the Tempe Canal Company." Arizona and the West, Autumn, 1965.

Logan, Michael F. Desert Cities. Pittsburgh: University of Pittsburgh Press, 2006.

Lyons, Bettina O'Neil. Zeckendorfs and Steinfelds, Merchant Princes of the Southwest. Tucson: Arizona Historical Society, 2008.

Luckingham, Bradford. Phoenix. Tucson: University of Arizona Press, 1989.

______. Minorities in Phoenix. Tucson: University of Arizona Press, 1994.

Lykes, Aimee. "Phoenix Women in the Development of Public Policy: Territorial Beginnings," 1982. Small Manuscript Collection, Arizona Historical Foundation. Tempe, Arizona

Luhrs, George H. N., Jr. The George H. N. Luhrs Family in Phoenix and Arizona 1847-1984. Phoenix: Jean Stroud Crane, 1988.

Marin, Christine. "Trinidad Meija Escalante Swilling, the Mother of Phoenix." Arizona Latina Trailblazers: Stories of Courage, Hope and Determination. Vol. 1, 2009. Phoenix: Latino Perspectives Media and Raul H. Castro Institute.

Mathews, Stanley R. and Elwyn L. Evans. " The Father of Phoenix." Journal of Arizona History, Autumn, 1986.

Mawn, Geoffrey P. "Phoenix, Arizona: Central City of the Southwest, 1870-1920." Ph. D. Dissertation. Arizona State University, 1974.

______. "Promoters, Speculators, and the Selection of the Phoenix Townsite." Arizona and the West, Fall, 1977.

McLaughlin, Herb and Dorothy. Phoenix 1870-1920 in Photographs. Phoenix: Herb and Dorothy McLaughlin, 1970.

McClintock, James H. Arizona. Chicago: The S. J. Clarke Publishing Company 1916.

Merrill, W. Earl. One Hundred Steps Down Mesa's Past. Mesa, Arizona: Lofgreen Printing Company, 1970.

McNamee, Gregory. Gila: The Life and Death of an American River. New York: Orion Books, 1994.

Napier, Rita. "Rethinking the Past, Reimagining the Future." Kansas History, Autumn, 2001.

Noble, David Grant, ed. The Hohokam. Santa Fe: School of American Research Press, 1991.

Orme, Charles. "The Saga of the Ormes in Arizona," 1968. Small Manuscript Collection. Arizona Historical Foundation. Tempe, Arizona.

Pagan, Eduardo. Historic Photos of Phoenix. Nashville, Tennessee: Turner Publishing Company, 2007.

Peffer, Louise. The Closing of the Public Domain. Palo Alto: Stanford University Press, 1951.

Peplow, Edward H.. Jr., ed. The Taming of the Salt. Phoenix: Salt River Project, 1979.

"Phoenix in '72 and '73." The Southwest Illustrated Magazine, June, 1895.

Pitzer, Gene. "Who Are Those Guys? Phoenix, Arizona Territory Law Enforcement 1870-1912," July, 2004.

Pry, Mark. The Life of Emil Ganz. Tempe, Arizona: Southwest Historical Series, February, 2001.

______. The Town on the Hassayampa. Wickenburg, Arizona: Desert Caballeros Western Museum, 1997.

Pueblo Grande Museum. "A River Ran Through It." Profiles No. 15, undated.

Reissner, Marc. Cadillac Desert. New York: Viking Penguin Books, 1986.

Robbins, Roy M. "Pre-Emption - A Frontier Triumph." The Mississippi Valley Historical Review, December, 1931.

Rochlin, Harriet and Fred. Pioneer Jews. Boston: Houghton Mifflin Company, 1984.

Rowe, Jeremy. "Arizona Pioneer Photographer George H. Rothrock." 2008. Web - www.vintagephoto.com.

Ryerson, Jennie S. "An Early History of Phoenix and the Salt River Valley from the Hohokam to 1891." M. A. Thesis, Arizona State College, Tempe, Arizona, 1948.

Salt River Project. Jack of All Trades: J. W. Swilling in the Arizona Territory. Phoenix: Salt River Project, 1992.

Smith, Dean. The Goldwaters of Arizona. Flagstaff, Arizona: Northland Press, 1986.

Smith, Henry Nash. "Rain Follows the Plow: The Notion of Increased Rainfall for the Great Plains, 1884-1880." Huntington Library Quarterly, February, 1947.

______. Virgin Land. Cambridge, Massachusetts: Harvard University Press, 1950.

Smith, Jared. Making Water Flow Uphill. Mesa, Arizona: Mesa Historical Society, 2004.

Smith, Karen Lynn. "From Town to City: A History of Phoenix, 1870-1912." M. A. Thesis, University of Southern California, Santa Barbara, 1978.

Sonnichsen, C. L. Tucson: The Life and Times of an American City. Norman: University of Oklahoma Press, 1982.

Steele, Volney. Bleed, Blister and Purge. Missoula, Montana: Mountain Press Publishing Company, 2005.

Stein, Pat. "Homesteading in Arizona, 1862-1940." Phoenix: Arizona State Historic Preservation Office, August, 1990.

Stegner, Wallace. Beyond the 100th Meridian. Boston: Houghton Mifflin, 1954.

Stocker, Joseph. "Jewish Roots in Arizona." Phoenix Jewish Community Council, 1954.

Swilling Files. Arizona Historical Foundation, Tempe, Arizona.

Tipton, Gary. "Men out of China." Journal of Arizona History, Autumn, 1977.

Veil, Fred. "Law and Justice in 19th Century Arizona Territory." Territorial Times, Fall, 2007.

______. "Murder on Whiskey Row." Paper presented at the Arizona History Convention. Prescott, Arizona. Spring, 2009.

Viola, Herman. Memoirs of Charles Veil. New York: Orion Books, 1993.

Wampler, Vance. Arizona Years of Courage. Phoenix: Quail Run Productions, 1984.

Wheeler, Keith. The Townsmen. Alexandria, Virginia: Time-Life Books, 1975.

White, Richard. It's Your Misfortune and None of My Own. Norman: University of Oklahoma Press, 1991.

Wildfang, Frederic B. and the Sharlot Hall Museum Archives. Prescott. Charleston, Chicago, et al.: Arcadia Publishing, 2006.

Wilson, Michael. Tragic Jack. Guilford, Connecticut: TwoDot, 2007.

Zarbin, Earl. "Henry Garfias, Phoenix's First City Marshal." The Journal of Arizona History, Spring, 2005.

______. The Swilling Legacy. Phoenix: Salt River Project, 1979.

______. "The Whole Was Done So Quietly, The Phoenix Lynchings of 1879." Journal of Arizona History, Winter, 1980.

______. Two Sides of the River: Salt River Valley Canals, 1867-1912. Phoenix: Salt River Project, 1997.

CREDITS

PAGE	TITLE	SOURCE
Cover	Lemon Office/Washington Street	AZ Archives
2	1867 Military Map of Arizona	AZ Archives
9	Jack Swilling	PPL
16	Hohokam Canal	Pueblo Grande Museum
17	Ingall's 1868 Survey	BLM
18-19	Turney Map	PPL
20	Cartwright Ditches	HF
35	Phoenix Townships	Karen Friend
39	John and Perlina Osborn	Osborn descendent
40	Columbus Gray	PPL
43	The Grays with Mary Green	PHM
48	Jasper and Sarah Cartwright	Sharlot Hall Museum
59	Wormser Office	AHF
72	John T. Alsap	AZ Archives
75	William and Lillie Hancock	AHF
76	Military Bounty Land Warrant	HF
83	Washington Street Scene	AZ Archives

Page	Title	Source
84	Hancock Store	PPL
85	Washington Street Cottonwoods	AHF
95	Goldman Store	AHF
97	Phoenix Herald	PPL
101	Phoenix Hotel	AZ Archives
102	Bank Exchange Hotel	AZ Archives
103	Rothrock Photo/Washington Street	AHF
103	Valencia Grocery	AHF
106	George Loring	AHF
117	Loring's Bazar	AHF
127	1873 Elementary School	AZ Archives
129	Central School	AHF
145	Enrique Garfias	Phoenix Police Museum
176	Phoenix Homesteaders Master List	Karen Friend
180	Phoenix Townsite	Karen Friend

AZ Archives - Arizona State Library and Archives
AHF - Arizona Historical Foundation
BLM - Bureau of Land Management
PHM - Phoenix History Museum
PPL - Phoenix Public Library
HF - Homesteading File